HIGHLAND BALLS

and

VILLAGE HALLS

G.W. Lockhart

By the same author:
The Scot and his Oats.
Luath Press. 1983.
Reprinted 1984, 1985.

HIGHLAND BALLS

AND

VILLAGE HALLS

G.W. Lockhart.

Luath Press Ltd.
Barr, Ayrshire.

To Helen, my wife.

*(And mony a happy dance, Chook, we've
had wi' ane anither.)*

Grateful acknowledgements are tendered to the following publishers and literary agents who have given permission for poems and prose passages to appear in this book:

Johnston and Bacon Ltd. for passage from *'The Tartans of the Clans and Families of Scotland'* by Sir Thomas Innes of Learney, Emeritus Lord Lyon King of Arms.

John Farquharson Ltd. for Passage from *'The General Danced at Dawn'* by George MacDonald Fraser.

Curtis Brown Group Ltd. for passage from *'Sunset Song'* reprinted by permission of Curtis Brown Ltd., on behalf of the Estate of James Leslie Mitchell. Copyright James Leslie Mitchell, 1932.

Curtis Brown Ltd. for passage from *'Cloud Howe'* reprinted by permission of Curtis Brown Ltd., on behalf of the Estate of Lewis Grassic Gibbon. Copyright James Leslie Mitchell, 1933.

Curtis Brown Ltd. for passage from *'The Trumpet in the Hall'* by Bernard Fergusson.

Kerr's Music Corporation Ltd. for verse from *'The Conversazione'* by Willie Kemp.

Brown, Son & Ferguson Ltd. for W.D. Crocker's Poem 'The Barn Dance'.

I little thought when I set out to write this book my journeys would extend so far or that I would experience such kindness and help from so many people. Encouragement I have been given in full measure, and to all those who have suffered my questioning, provided leads and put themselves about to dig up information which seemed to me pertinent, I express my gratitude and the hope that they will enjoy many years of happy dancing.

In particular, I express my grateful thanks to:

Miss Florence Adams of Motherwell.
The Staff of Angus Libraries and Museums.
Andrew Bathgate of Longniddry.
Mrs. Marion Campbell of Millden, Glenesk.
John Drewry of Aberdeen.
Major Michael Drummond-Brady of Hopetoun House, South Queensferry.
The Staff of the Music Room of Edinburgh Central Library.
Sir Ewan Forbes of Brux, Aberdeenshire.
Ian Gent of Linlithgow.
Charles Gore of Port Na Mine, Taynuilt, Argyll.
Col. Tom Lamb of The Burn, Edzell, Angus.
Miss Dorothy Leurs of Edinburgh.
Lt. Col. Stuart MacBain, R.H.Q., Royal Scots.
Ian MacDonald of Kirkintilloch.
Miss Iona MacDonald of Portree.
Jim MacLeod of Dunblane.
Gibbie McIntosh of Colquhonnie Hotel, Strathdon.
Miss Mary Milne of Banchory.
John Mortimer of The Assembly Rooms, Edinburgh.
A.J. Munro of Atholl Estates, Blair Atholl.
J.I.D. Pottinger, M.V.O., Lyon Clerk and Keeper of the Records.
Percy Rodgers of Edinburgh.
Robbie Shepherd of B.B.C. Radio Scotland.
Peter Maxwell Stuart of Traquair.

Special thanks are due to my wife who, with faultless loyalty, has checked proofs, refrained from commenting on papers scattered all over the place and managed the surprising amount of adminstrative chores the preparation of a book like this requires. David Dingwall has been my Pancho and aided in a multitude of ways. Once again that fine Border artist, Jim Coltman of Hawick, has come to my aid, and I am immeasurably in his debt for the delightful sketches he has produced for this book. To these three I add affection to my thanks.

The Ball held in Edinburgh to celebrate the 50th anniversary of the Royal
Scottish Country Dance Society.
Photo: Scotsman Publications, Edinburgh.

CONTENTS

INTRODUCTION

For nought can cheer the heart sae weel,
As can a canty Highland reel;
It even vivifies the heel
> *To skip and dance:*
Lifeless is he wha canna feel
> *Its influence.*

'The Daft Days' — Robert Fergusson (1750—1774)

'There's nothing like a Broun's Reel,' my father would say, and then in an undertone which emphasised his enjoyment, 'There's just nothing like it!' The sweat on his brow bespoke his feelings. For as long as I could remember, country dancing had been his love, indeed his passion. At weddings and other social occasions I had watched, as a youngster, his stilted movement round the floor to the strains of a modern waltz or foxtrot. But when the chord was struck for an Eightsome, Strip the Willow or Petronella, the strong, square form was transformed, as if by magic, into a figure of vigour and daintiness. It was a living example of man matching his environment, and proof that, in a Calvinistic world, enjoyment demanded at the end of a night that all energy had been drained from the body even though the spirit remained exhilarated.

But, of course, he was not alone of his generation. In keeping with we will never know how many thousands of young men and girls, he had cycled or walked countless miles to dances in village halls. On entry, the jackets would be hung on the nearest convenient nail and

1

The Juniper Green Dancers performing four reels of four, Real Madrid
Football Club Stadium. *Photo: Percy Rodgers, Edinburgh.*

from then on it would be frenzied activity as dance followed
dance. Not for them todays's restricted programme of sixteen
dances. The dancers themselves indicated the duration of the
entertainment and it would be a dull evening without more than one
Eightsome, Broun's Reel or Lancers. The flickering oil-lamps on
the bicycles danced their rhapsody on the country roads home, and if
there was only two or three hours sleep in bed before the incumbent
was roused at five by the clockwork alarm, there would be much to
talk about the next day: the quality of the fiddling, the feed of stovies,
and perhaps, too, a comment on the lass given a hurl home on the
cross-bar.

Although brought up in a home where the carpet was frequently
lifted when visitors were in, for the Lancers and Quadrilles, to begin
with I took a fairly detached view of the proceedings. As a boy,

unlike my young female relatives and friends, I was reluctant to push myself into a set made up of adults, and, of course, it would have been unthinkable for the youngsters to dance on their own. The music was pleasure enough, and with the early recognition that the onlooker sees more of the game came also the realisation that dancing eased the cares away, and, in the harsher clime of my boyhood, served as a rejuvenating tonic as well as providing honest, clean, and not least, inexpensive enjoyment. By the time I was twelve, I could dance comfortably at any homely occasion.

It was to be at school, a few seasons later, that some undesirable traits developed in my dancing. Fourth year boys were admitted to the school dance, and it was the duty of the gym teacher to instruct the boys how to dance properly and, what was considered much more important, the rudiments of ballroom etiquette: how ladies should be

Dancing in the street.   Tong, Lewis, 1928.
Photo: National Museum of Antiquities of Scotland

3

Jim Cameron's Band.

Still going strong — the great Jim MacLeod Band.
Photos: Dundee Courier and Advertiser.

invited to dance, how they should be treated on the floor, how they should be returned to their seats and thanked.   Looking back, I thank old Mac for his efforts, but at that time, going through the period of being obnoxious which is common to so many boys, my feelings were an amalgam of fear, if not hate, of the female sex, and sheer bloody revolution against such a structured and formal society.   At practice in the gym, I was happy to keep my line straight and, under Mac's watchful eyes, no robustness would enter the dancing.   But *'birling'* (or *'burling*, a couthier and more expressive term) had become my speciality and in my mind's eye was sustained the ambitious dream of *'birling'* into a state of fear and submission those female teachers who made the life of an inattentive schoolboy such misery.   I was strong enough to do it with my aunts: why not with my teachers?

The school dance was a grand affair.   With astonishment I discovered that some classmates actually had dinner jackets (and remember these were the days when sixteen year old boys wore shorts to school.)   The girls wore dresses that enhanced them in ways that gym slips failed to do, and some of them were actually quite presentable.   The boys, maintaining a strained composure, stood down one side of the hall, while the girls, affecting a sophistication designed to conceal the dread that they would not be invited to dance, grouped themselves down the other, the more brazen aligning themselves in the forefront.   No-man's land was occupied by the teachers who would make sure no girl was left out if there was a boy available, and woe betide any youth the next school-day who willingly allowed a girl to remain unpartnered, however pimply and ugly she might be.

My target for the night was my language teacher, not because I disliked her, rather more because I hated French.   She accepted my invitation to dance a Strip the Willow, and having announced to my friends how I would have her legs off the floor, there was a rush to join my set.   Perhaps I indicated my intentions too early; perhaps she had experienced it all before.   As I worked her down the men's side of the

dance her face displayed nothing but happiness and peace with the world. At the end of the line we started to birl. Our arms were linked hard and as I increased the speed the smile on her face seemed to grow, even if the eyes reverted more to their classroom stare. Round and round we went. This was to be no mandatory turn for two bars, and I was conscious of cries of encouragement from the sidelines as we gyrated with fury. Then suddenly something akin to fear grasped me. My feet were losing their grip while she, firmly anchored to the floor, was increasing speed, her smile widening and her eyes ever hardening. Desperately I released myself from her hold, and, retaining what composure I could, gratefully accepted the arm offered to me by the girl at the bottom of the set. We were now out of time with the band and the dance finished in shambolic fashion. I returned the teacher to her seat and she thanked me graciously for the dance. She spoke no word of admonition then or ever. But she knew she had conquered me, indeed had rubbed my nose in it. I never respected any teacher more.

It was after I left the Army and was settling down in my first job near Kirriemuir that I got caught up in the great heyday of country dancing.   Several nights a week the radio blared its country dance music.   It is doubtful if there was ever such a richness of top bands as moved around Angus and its neighbouring counties in the late forties and early fifties.   The apparently endless list included Jimmy Shand, Ian Powrie, the Hawthorn Band and my special favourite, Jim Cameron.   Cameron's sound was, of course, unique because of the inclusion in the band of a cornet player, and I still maintain that the band's rendering of 'Caddam Woods' gave us the most exciting record ever made.   Sadly, my old '78' was worn thin by countless revolutions before it finally disappeared in the course of a 'flitting'.   I like to think it was appropriated by someone who regarded himself as a connoisseur of Scots music.   Amongst the composers of that era, Angus Fitchet and Adam Rennie stood perhaps a shade higher than the rest.

At the Rugby Clubs', Former Pupils' and similar balls I attended, the country dancing held equal standing with ballroom dances such as the modern waltz, quickstep, tango and so on, while the Schottische and Gay Gordons would find their way into the inevitable Paul Jones.   It was a comfortable balance, allowing opportunity for letting one's hair down and closer proximity to the girl of one's choice.   Dancing pumps were never seen, although there were rumours that such effeminate and stage gear were worn by men who attended peculiar dancing classes, behind closed doors, where yeoching and birling were banned.   Indeed, I was to be nearer fifty than forty before I bought my first pair of pumps.   Even today, as I put them on, I am still susceptible to the conscience prick that they are 'sissy'.   But more of that later.

As my work meanderings entailed the taking up of residence in various parts of England, I followed the exile's fairly common practice of joining the nearest St. Andrew's Society or Caledonian Club, and it was this that first brought home to me the international appeal of Scottish country dancing.   I marvelled at the enthusiasm shown by people of many other nationalities. The English colonel of one Territorial Army regiment I served with was so fanatical that on Mess Nights he would order us away from our drinks to make up sets. And if you know anything about the T.A. you will place no small value on his moral courage. But nevertheless I slowly drifted from the dancing scene. When I returned to Scotland, times and dancing habits had changed. Philosophically I accepted the change. Other interests and pursuits came to the fore, although the music itself could not be ignored, and the piles of records on top of the piano continued to rise. I did not know the best had yet to come.

For more years than I care to remember Edinburgh has been my Mecca. Boyhood holidays to the capital to stay with relatives, visits to the Zoo, the castle and the Royal Mile, fostered within me the conviction that my life would never be complete unless I had ready access to it. Above all, Murrayfield on an 'International Day' possessed a magic and expectancy that exceeded the thrill of hanging up one's Christmas stocking. A few years after my return to Scotland, a number of unexpected happenings caused the fates to be kind to me and I was able to live near the most delightful city in the world, and savour all it has to offer.

A concert to be given by the Edinburgh Strathspey and Reel Society warranted my attention, and I joined the capacity audience in the Usher Hall for a delightful evening. But more than that — I experienced a conversion that smacked of the Road to Damascus. On to the stage of that magnificent auditorium came the demonstration team of the Edinburgh Branch of the Royal Scottish Country Dance Society. Never before had I seen dancing of such quality: indeed, I did not think such perfection possible. I forgave the men their wearing of pumps and left the concert fired with the ambition to return to dancing and to find out more about this, to me, rather unknown Society. My enquiries bore magnificent fruit. Scottish country dancing was not dead; it had, in a peculiar way, gone underground. Hundreds of clubs and classes existed, all devoted to learning far more

dances than I ever thought there could possibly be, and dancing in a
style that contrasted with my habits as a trade does with an art.   If
at times the art seemed more important than having fun, it would be a
small price to pay for the sheer enjoyment of moving to the most
compelling music in the world.   So, a pair of pumps was bought, a
beginners' class was joined and an unlearning, as well as a learning,
experience began.   Now, with superiority, I could look down my
nose at those buffoons of my age who tried to keep themselves fit by
jogging.   I could be fit, mentally as well as physically, in the most
delectable and exhilarating way possible.

And there my introduction must end.   In *'Sunset Song'* Lewis
Grassic Gibbon gives a wonderful description that takes me back to
my early dancing days:

'But then Chae cried 'Strip the Willow', and they all
lined up, and the melodeon played bonnily in Chae's
hands, and Long Rob's fiddle-bow was darting and
glimmering, and in two minutes, there wasn't a cold
soul in Blawearie barn.   Chris found herself in the
arms of the minister, he could dance like a daft
young lad.   And as he swung her round and around
he opened his mouth and cried "Hooch! Hooch!" and
so did the red Highlander, McIvor, "Hooch!" career-
ing by with fat Kirsty Strachan, real scared-like, she
looked, clipped round the waist.'

It is a far cry from those days to where and what I practise
today.   But the urge to dance is the same, and the music is the
same.   What Scot would ask for anything more?

The Michie Band played regularly in Glen Esk around the turn of the century.
Photo: Glenesk Folk Museum.

THE STORY OF THE DANCE

He blew them rants sae lively, schottisches, reels an' jigs,
The foalie flung his muckle legs an' capered ower the rigs,
The grey-tailed futtrat bobbit oot to hear his ain strathspey,
The bawd cam' loupin' through the corn to 'Clean Pease Strae'.
The Whistle — Charles Murray (1864-1941)

There is little doubt that in Scotland, dancing is in the blood. Whatever the occasion, it seems the Scot can find an excuse to get his feet moving. Even the least gregarious need little urging to make up a set, while, shy, introverted characters develop lion-like presences when performing their solo-setting in the middle of an Eightsome Reel. As reference to the world-wide list of clubs in the Royal Scottish Country Dance Society's year-book indicates, the Scot does not leave his native dances behind him when settling or journeying overseas. Indeed, his nationalism expands, and he dances more than ever, showing no surprise that the local population, whatever their race, creed or colour, seek to join his frolics with an almost equal vigour. It appears completely natural to him that the Gurkhas, Sikhs, Malays and Arabs should want to learn how to play the pipes.

The Scot has danced in prisoner of war camps, in castles and cottage kitchens, in night schools and day schools, in defeat and in victory. Some time ago I attended a shoot on a bitterly cold November day. As we stood at the roadside waiting for lunch to arrive, our blue noses resembled lamps outside a police station. From the inside of a game bag, one of the 'keepers' produced the smallest of concertinas. Within seconds, it seemed, the air was alive with 'yeochs' as tackety and wellington boots broke the frost in a rousing Eightsome. Dancing at christenings and weddings is common enough, but Fergusson reminds us that at one time funerals, too, were

an excuse to get into action:
> *I dwall amang the caller springs*
> *That weet the Land O' Cakes,*
> *And aften tune my canty strings*
> *At bridals and late-wakes.*

Why should Scottish country dancing be the most popular form of traditional dancing throughout the world?   It is an interesting question.   No doubt the fact that it is performed in social groups, or sets, is a factor, but this is not unique.   Portugese dancing follows this pattern but has never gained much acceptance outwith that country. American square dancing has a vibrancy and exudes bonhomie; yet prevalent as the Americans are today, all over the globe, and much as the free world is influenced by things American, from chewing-gum to jeans, a ho-down would still be something for a European to regard as a tourist attraction.   To explain the commitment of races from Japan to Venezuala to Scottish country dancing demands, at least, some analysis.

It was probably in the fourteenth century that set dancing of some form originated in Scotland, but reference to it is scant until the sixteen hundreds.   From then on its growth was documented, and it is interesting to note that many dances, such as 'The Gates of Edinburgh' and 'The Red House' devised quite early in the eighteenth century, are still danced today, although little dance music was published before 1750.

In 1746, the Act of Proscription was passed, aimed at eliminating Highland culture.   As a byproduct, it opened the door for the fiddle to become the national instrument of Scotland.   While no-one would ever deny the excellence of the marriage of the pipes with some of the great dances, such as 'Bonnie Anne', equally, no-one would gainsay that the fiddle is the ideal musical instrument for indoor country dancing.   The popularity of fiddling and dancing grew cheek by jowl in the second half of the eighteenth century, as Scotland entered her golden age.   And it was at this time that the population of the towns

The great 32-some Reel at the Gathering of the Clans, Meadowbank, Edinburgh, 1977.

Photo: Miss Dorothy Leurs, Edinburgh.

began to express their increasing sophistication at dance assemblies. Mrs. Cockburn, poetess, inveterate lettter writer and the most famous hostess of her day, recorded, around 1760:

'Next day I went to the assembly. Never was so handsome an assembly. There were seven sets — one all quality ladies and all handsome; one called the maiden set, for they admitted no married women; one called the heartsome set, which was led off by Lady Christian Erskine, in which danced Mrs. Horn, Suff Johnston, Anne Keith; Bess St. Clair and Lady Dunmore humbly begged to stand at the foot, which was granted. Suff was my bedfellow all night, and is just gone.'

And later, in a letter expressing her pleasure at the 'Cottar's Saturday Night', she writes that:

'The town is at present agog with the ploughman poet. The man will be spoiled, if he can spoil; but he keeps his simple manners, and is quite sober. No doubt he will be at the Hunters' Ball tomorrow, which has made all women and milliners mad. Not a gauze cap under two guineas — many ten, twelve, etc.'

The nineteenth century gave Scottish dances the opportunity to test their mettle and resilience against the ballroom products of Europe. The Quadrilles, Waltz and Polka captured a dancing public's imagination, and, at least for a while, reels and jigs suffered relegation, although the strathspey, especially in its foursome reel form, managed to hold its popularity, particularly in the country areas. The Scots at first accepted these continental introductions, before either discarding them or absorbing them into their own mode of dancing. The Quadrilles, of course, can still occasionally be enjoyed today in certain outlying places; the waltz has produced its derivations such as Waltz Country Dance, and the Polka, overtaken by the Poussette as a progression, steadfastly refuses to die. Not everyone, however, welcomed the innovations. Lady Nairne animatedly defends the old dances in her rumbustious poem 'County Meeting'.

WHEN WARK IS OWER AN SUPPER DUNE THE BOTHY BAND COMES ON THE SCENE
AT JIGS STRATHSPEYS, AN HIELAN REELS THERE'S FEW CAN BEAT OOR BOTHY CHIELS

A Bothy Band.
Photo: National Museum of Antiquities of Scotland.

> *But ne'er ye fash, gang thro' the reel,*
> *The country-dance, ye dance sae weel,*
> *An' ne'er let waltz or dull quadrille*
> *Spoil our County Meeting.*

The word *'Quadrilles'* naturally conjures up the word *'Lancers'* for these two rather similar dances are inexorably linked together. But be warned! Because there are so many local variations, to get up to the Lancers today is to put oneself at considerable risk. Attending a Sheepdog Trial Dance in a remote glen (it started after eleven o'clock when the beer tent closed), the Lancers was demanded and I found myself in a set with three enormous shepherds, partnered by wives only marginally inferior in physique, from different but neighbouring glens. Each had his own version of the dance; each was convinced his version was the only true one; each intended the set would conform. It was not an experience I would like to relive. But such behaviour, of course, is most uncommon. Scottish country dancing is fundamentally ballroom dancing and it implies elegance as well as enjoyment:

> *The room whirled and coloured*
> *and figured itself with dancers.*

as Norman McCaig sallies in his *'Country Dance'*.

There is a completeness about a Scottish country dance programme that produces a feeling of achievement as well as satisfaction. It changes from the fast movement of the reel or the more moderately phased jig to the stately strathspey. There is an appeal to both sexes; the men can be masculine and the ladies feminine. It is easy to start country dancing because there are few basic steps, but just as the competent golfer gets drugged on lowering his handicap, so does the country dancer get hooked on learning more movements and progressions, not to mention more dances, while all the time seeking to polish the performance.

There is one further aspect of Scottish country dancing to be identified at this point. And it is an important aspect, as it explains, to at least some extent, the emotional attachment the Scot has to his native dances.   The dances, be they reels, jigs, hornpipes or strathspeys, are enjoyed at all levels of society.   Whilst not a classless society, the divisions that can be found in Scotland are not so significant as in many other countries.   The clan system had something to do with this, as had, and has, the natural independence of the Scot.

There is thus something important to record and keep alive and just as, last century, the Scottish dances had to withstand the introduction and challenge of dances from the Continent, so one expects that our native dances will not be overwhelmed this century by the new styles which have made their mark, but that they will continue in the years ahead to provide pleasure for all who respond to the strains of our traditional music by wanting to dance.

THE STRATHSPEY
AND
THE STRATHSPEY KING

What needs there be sae great a fraise
Wi' dringing dull Italian lays,
I wadna gie our ain Strathspeys
For half a hunder score o' them.
     'Tullochgorum' — John Skinner (1721–1807)

There is an emotional attachment to the Strathspey.   Its distinctive music encourages a desire to give one's all to the dance.   The Reel provides the opportunity to let the hair down, but the Strathspey is all about good manners and graciousness, precision and elegance, moulded on to some of the most beautiful tunes ever written.   The Strathspey both warms and delights.

It would be nice to prove that the Strathspey was first performed somewhere in the vast region that has given it its name, but history at times can be unhelpful.   Certainly links with the region are very strong, and writers of the eighteenth and nineteenth centuries commented that the dance was performed in its purest fashion on Speyside.

James Scott Skinner, Scotland's greatest fiddle composer, is quite positive about its origins.   Writing in his *'Guide to Bowing'* he says:
    'The Strathspey undoubtedly had its origins on Speyside. These effusions of nature which bear the stamp of antiquity are mostly written in what may be called the pipe scale with its characteristic flat seventh.'

19

Scott Skinner, Scotland's greatest composer and fiddler, in characteristic pose.

Photo: Miss Mary Milne, Banchory.

This scale seems to have gone to the brain of the men of earlier days — hence such wild and distinctive tunes as *'Tullochgorum'* and *'Reel of Tulloch'*. It can be argued that the Strathspey grew out of the Reel. They are both four-four time and the steps of both dances indicate a common root. It is not difficult to imagine a preference for a slow dance or a quick dance arising. But the division between the two had certainly been accomplished before the mid-1700's, and perhaps much earlier, although there is an interesting suggestion that as ladies gave up the wearing of hooped skirts towards the end of the eighteenth century, and were thus able to dance faster, the division widened to allow the development of two more distinct dancing styles. At that time, Creech, the famous Edinburgh worthy and publisher, was able to describe the Reel as riotous and the Strathspey as sprightly.

Burns recorded in a letter that *'many of our Strathspeys ancient and modern give me exquisite enjoyment.'* In his later years, Burns was to put words to some old Strathspey tunes (*Green grow the Rashes* is a good example) which ensured their continuing popularity. But certainly the second half of the eighteenth century was a most prolific period as far as the composing of Strathspeys was concerned.

A study of dance programmes over the later years of the last century and the earlier ones of the present century suggests a falling off in affection for the Strathspey. It is difficult to give a reason for this. Perhaps it was not rumbustious enough for a population which sought sweat and excitement from its dancing. Certainly it is the writer's childhood recollection that at village dances there would not be more than one or two local favourites such as *Monymusk* and *The Glasgow Highlanders,* and there was no strong demand for a greater number. But then it is doubtful if many of the dancing population had any idea of the hundreds of dances which make up our dancing heritage. The position today, of course, in country dancing circles, is much brighter, with the Strathspey occupying a full share of any programme.

Recent years, too, have seen the introduction of some new Strathspeys, many built on old tunes, which give the greatest pleasure to dance. Individual talent arises in every age, and today one acknowledges the composition talent of John Drewry of Aberdeen who is providing so much pleasure with his beautiful Strathspeys like *'The Duchess Tree'* and *'The Bonnie Lass O' Bon Accord.'*

James Scott Skinner was born in 1843 in the little Deeside town of Banchory. Of his formative and early years we know remarkably little, save that as a member of one Dr. Mark's orchestra he performed at Buckingham Palace and later at Balmoral. He seems to have had a devotion to the Royal family, sending both lines of verse and music to Queen Victoria and the Duke of Edinburgh. It must be remembered that Skinner was a professional dancer before achieving fame as a fiddler and composer. His dance schools were run over wide tracts of the North-east, and catered for the young of both rich and poor — both of whom were liable to receive a rap on the head with his fiddle bow. His classes were large, which may explain his emphasis on figures rather than techniques, but etiquette was never neglected. Even at this early stage of his musical career his flair for the unusual showed through, and many of his classes would finish their season with fancy dress balls.

As the years passed, his ability as a fiddler received greater recognition, and he had no inhibitions about extending his repertoire to include the classics. Thanks to the technology of our age, we are able to hear recordings made by Skinner late in his career, and appreciate the beauty of his playing.

To great acclaim, concert followed concert, until he became a household name in the North of Scotland. The 'Dundee Advertiser' of 1st November 1881 stated that 'Mr. Skinner is a musician to the manner born and his ideas are in loving sympathy with the very essence of purely Scotch dance melody.' Perhaps more genuinely illustrative of his talents were the lines submitted by a newspaper reader:

I had a nicht, an' only ane,
Wi' James Scott Skinner,
Nae lang ago in Aberdeen,
Wi' James Scott Skinner.
An' sic a nicht I never saw,
Nor spent afore wi' great nor sma'
For I could hardly win awa'
Frae James Scott Skinner.

Another newspaper reader in the same year, in a letter to the 'Aberdeen Weekly Free Press', where he shields behind the pseudonym of 'An Old Deeside Man', recounts a story of Scott Skinner's father (who was also a fiddler and dancing master) at a wedding.   It was at a time when weddings, being frequently held in the open air, were an occasion for the high-spirited letting-off of guns.   While he was taking part in these festivities, the firelock of Skinner Senior burst, damaging the fingers of his left hand.   Such was his natural ability that he was able to transfer the bowing to his left hand while fingering with his right.   If it can be said that the talents of the father were handed down the line to the son, it can also be said that the son did not forget the father.   One of Scott Skinner's compositions was to be entitled *'The Left-handed Fiddler'.*

Dancing in those days required stamina from fiddlers and dancers alike.   Sets were not limited in number, and there is one known occasion when Skinner played non-stop for twenty couples to complete *The Merry Lads o' Ayr.*

However, today the name of James Scott Skinner is predominantly recalled for his compositions which have become the accepted tunes for many Strathspey dances.   It must be remembered that he did not write with dancing in mind.   He wrote for concert purposes, enjoyment, or to provide the basis for a song.   But his output of music was prodigious, with over six hundred tunes published and many others passed on to friends in manuscript form.   His first collection, the *'Miller o' Hirn'* was published in 1881, to be followed by the Elgin,

Logie, Harp and Claymore Collections in due course. It is interesting and, perhaps to us today, rather difficult to understand why some of his compositions were designated either singly 'Strathspey' or 'Highland Schottische' or the dual 'Strathspey or Schottische'. But the strength of the melodies, which is the hallmark of his work, has encouraged adaptation in recent years. *'The Bonnie Lass o' Bon Accord',* for example, dedicated to one James Walker, President of Aberdeen Musical Association, was written as a Solo song or Marching air. Thirty years ago, regrettably not with the original words, *'Bon Accord'* was often heard in variety theatres. It has lasted as a Gay Gordons favourite. But today, it is regarded as one of the most beautiful of all Strathspeys. The Quadrilles, too, claimed Skinner's attention. The *'Balmoral and Ettrick Vale Quadrilles'* were well received introductions, but the mind boggles at the thought of performing his *'Logie Singing Quadrille',* which required the singing of no less than fourteen verses while dancing!

The contribution of James Scott Skinner to the world of Scottish music was immense. No disservice to that which he gave is intended if his public relations promotions are recalled. His title of 'The Strathspey King' was self-assumed. His *'Talisker Schottische',* with a cover showing two Highlanders partaking of *'the fine speerit of Talisker'* was a leading advertisement of his day.

Skinner died in Aberdeen in 1927 — the last of the great fiddle composers. In earlier years he had written about Burns: *'All other Scottish poetry is as moonlight unto sunlight and as water unto wine. It is impossible to rival him and dangerous to imitate him.'* Perhaps that last sentence might be a fitting epitaph for James Scott Skinner.

BLAIR CASTLE

I ne'er lo'ed a dance but on Athole's green,
I ne'er lo'ed a lassie but my dorty Jean;
Sair, sair against my will did I bide sae lang awa',
An' my heart was aye in Athole's green at Carlisle ha'
The Bonnie Brier Bush — Baroness Nairne (1766-1845)

The ballroom at Blair Castle is warm and impressive. The warmth comes from its heavy timbering and panelling with the large and well-known painting of Neil Gow in his tight tartan knee-breeches and hose making a unique contribution to the scene. The minstrel gallery is near enough to the floor to establish cosiness between dancers and musicians. The impressiveness, of course, comes from the historic accoutrements around the room, for Blair Castle is the seat of the Duke of Atholl, Chief of the Murrays and the only person in Britain with the right to a private army, the Atholl Highlanders. Thus above the dancers are arrayed the colours of the Regiment and a host of antlers, spears and warlike paraphernalia. Add to this some magnificent oil portraits of former Dukes and a Landseer stalking scene, and it is not difficult to conjure up in the mind a picture of Scotland's history.

The ballroom was added to the Castle in 1877, some thirty years after Queen Victoria and Prince Albert visited the Castle and enjoyed a night's dancing in the riding school.

Royalty's first visit to the ballroom was paid by King Edward VII. His Majesty, it is recorded, was accustomed to dancing all night, a feat which more than taxed some of the musicians who had, in addition to their social obligations, to complete a full day's work on the estate. There is a tale told of Piper MacPherson who was summoned to play for the reels after a particularly arduous day on the

25

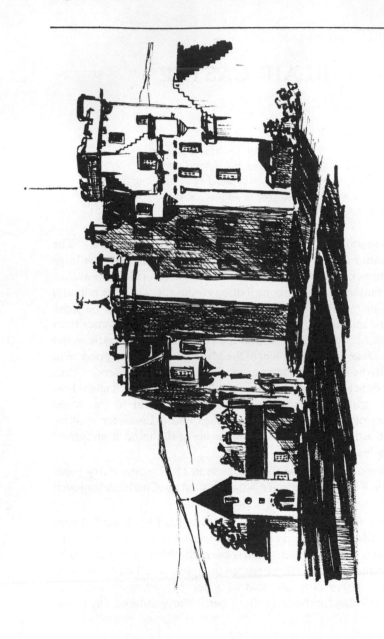

hills.   The poor piper not only fell asleep on some rugs after playing for the King, but two or three times had to be forcibly roused to consciousness to meet His Majesty's demand for more reels.

A look through any dance catalogue will show how many dances are associated with the Castle and the surrounding neighbourhood. *'The Duke of Atholl's Reel, Duchess of Atholl's Slipper* and *Struan Robertson's Reel'* were firm favourites.   Reels were, and indeed still are, danced to the pipes with the fiddlers taking over for the Quadrilles, Strathspeys and continental introductions.   Today the ballroom houses many private functions, but the most important dance of the year is the Atholl Highlanders' Ball.

Sadly the Atholl Gathering Ball is no long a regular calendar event.   Until 1857 the ball to celebrate this meeting of the Murrays was held in a tent.   That year, however, a local hostelry, the Blair Inn (now known as the Atholl Arms Hotel) built a large room for dancing and the ball was held there every year until the gathering moved into the new ballroom in the Castle in 1877.   The last Gathering Ball was held in the ballroom in 1913.   During the war the ballroom was used as a hospital ward but the ball was not resumed at the end of hostilities.

No story of dancing at Blair Castle, of course, would be complete without reference to the great Neil Gow, fiddler to three Dukes of Atholl and father of Nathaniel and grandfather of Neil Junior who inherited much of his talent.   Gow was born at Inver near Dunkeld in 1727 and his extraordinary talent with the fiddle was recognised at an early age by the Atholl family.   Through the family he was introduced to many members of the nobility and employed at fashionable dances.   His fame soon reached London where he was frequently called upon to play Country Dance music.   When playing, we are told, he would give sudden bellows during quick tunes which seemed to electrify the dancers and inspire them with new life and energy.   In his time, Gow was without equal in the playing of reels and strathspeys and he ranks amongst the greatest as a composer.   His laments in particular are indescribably beautiful and are much performed at fiddlers' rallies. Nearly a hundred tunes are accredited to him, and his son Nat, who wrote '*Caller Herrin'*', was to pass on the great Gow talent in due course to his own son Neil Junior.

Elizabeth Grant in her '*Memoirs of a Highland Lady*' recounts how excited she would become when Gow was invited to play for the family when they were stopping overnight at the Inn at Inver *en route* to their home in Rothiemurchus. Later pages in the autobiography tell something of the reputation Gow had established in his lifetime:
> 'When next we passed our boundary river the handsome bridge was built over it at Dunkeld, the little inn was done up, a fine hotel where the civillest of landlords reigned, close to the bridge, received all travellers; and Neil Gow was dead, the last of our bards — no one again will ever play the Scotch music as he did. His sons in the quick measures were perhaps his equals, they gave force and spirit and fine execution to strathspeys and reels, but they never gave the slow, the tender airs with the real feeling for beauty their father had. Nor can anyone now hope to revive a style passing away. A few true fingers linger amongst us, but this generation will see the last of them.'

Gow, as is well known, had a great liking for whisky. The story is told of Gow wending his way home from playing at a function at Blair Castle when he fell in with a friend who commiserated with him on the distance he had to walk. 'It's not the length of the road that worries me,' Gow is reputed to have replied, 'It's the breadth.' Ironically, the Chartist Press, which insisted strongly on the social evils of alcohol, adopted Gow's '*Farewell to Whisky*' as its theme tune. Burns, during his Highland tour, met Gow and described him as a short, stout-built Highland figure with grey hair on an honest social brow. Burns penned the words to be seen today on the plaque on the wall of Gow's cottage at Inver near Dunkeld:

> *'Nae fabled wizard's wand I trow*
> *Had e'er the magic art o' Gow*
> *When in a wave he draws his bow*
> *Across his wondrous fiddle.'*

Blair Castle, of course, is the home of that wonderful and invigorating drink Athole Brose.   This is a concoction of genius, made from whisky, oatmeal and honey, and is virtually guaranteed to put life and mettle into the heels of all dancers.   One wonders if perhaps Neil Gow knew of it, and whether its considerable powers helped him in his remarkable feats of fiddling.

THE ASSEMBLY ROOMS, EDINBURGH

Nancy's to the assembly gone
To hear the fops a-chattering
And Willie he has followed her
To win her love by flattering.
Nancy's to the Assembly Gone — Mrs. Cockburn (1712-1794)

The Caledonian Hunt Ball of 11th January 1787 marked the opening of the George Street Assembly Rooms. It was a magnificent occasion. The ladies were dressed in the height of fashion wearing gowns of different coloured satins and Spanish or turban style hats. The Assembly Room itself, flanked by the large East and West drawing rooms and boasting large chandeliers, was considered to be the most elegant in Britain. Truly, the residents of the New Town could now consider themselves to be at the centre of sophistication.

Sadly, Burns, who was in Edinburgh at the time of the ball, does not seem to have been present, but he does make reference to it in one of his letters. The Assembly Room in due course was to have close association with the giants of literature, but one would give much to know what thoughts went through Burns's head as he watched the ladies and gentlemen of the day enter their sedan chairs to be carried off for their evening's entertainment.

The George Street Assembly Rooms were not the first to grace the Edinburgh social scene. According to Chambers's *'Traditions of Edinburgh'* published in 1823, the first place were the fashionables held their dancing assemblies was in premises in the Bow. Graham's *'Social Life of Scotland in the Eighteenth Century'*, however, indicated a behavior at those early functions which would scarcely

gain the approbation of the genteel folk of Edinburgh today:
'Each partner had been chosen by a gentleman before the ball,
the selection being made at some private party, when all the fans
were placed in a cocked hat, and the owner of the fan picked out
became the partner for the night — each having a shrewd guess
who was the fair owner of the fan he took.   The tickets were
then bought by the gentleman, who sometimes had one or two
oranges stowed away in his coat pocket for the refreshment of
his lady, who sucked them during pauses of conversation and
intervals in the dance — a succulent process which she varied by
presenting to her nose delicate pinches of snuff which she
extracted from the dainty snuff-box hanging by her side.   The
customary price for the ticket was two shillings and sixpence,
not defraying the modest expenses of tea and coffee which

were consumed in the card-room and the proceeeds of the ball were devoted to charity — especially to the new Royal Infirmary, which was enlisting popular interest.'

The ordinary people of the capital seem to have taken some time to accept the assemblies as part of the social scene, but the amiable Allan Ramsay, as expected, enjoined the population of the capital to rally round:

> *Dear Em'brugh! shaw thy gratitude,*
> *And of sic friends make sure,*
> *Wha strive to make our minds less rude,*
> *And help our wants to cure;*
> *Acting a generous part and good,*
> *In bounty to the poor;*
> *Sic virtues, if right understood,*
> *Should ev'ry heart allure.*

It is an interesting thought that, whilst the townspeople of Edinburgh were railing against dancing, their counterparts in the country were considering it their normal mode of relaxation.

In a later Assembly Room built in 1766 in Bell's Wynd, the standards of good behaviour were maintained — *'No lady to be admitted in a night-gown and no gentleman in boots'* — but by this time, as Sir Alexander Boswell pointed out, the dancers were beginning to become caricatured:

> *Then were the days of modesty of mien!*
> *Stays for the fat, and quilting for the lean;*
> *The ribboned stomacher, in many a plait,*
> *Upheld the chest, and dignified the gait,*
> *Some Venus, brightest planet of the train,*
> *Moved in a lustering halo, propped with a cane.*

However, the Bell's Wynd Assembly Room was to be found too dingy and inconvenient, and building work started on the George Street Assembly Rooms in 1784.

The new Assembly Room was used regularly for dancing during Scotland's Golden Age, with subscription books available from a Mr. William Sanderson, a merchant in the luckenbooths —the name given to that part of the High Street opposite St. Giles Cathedral where goldsmiths and silversmiths and bookbinders had their locked (lucken) booths, as opposed to the open booths of other traders.

The year 1822 was to see the new Assembly Room provide the setting for one of the most glittering occasions of all time. Following his coronation the year before, King George IV decided to be the first Hanoverian monarch to set foot in Scotland. To Sir Walter Scott, who had attended the crowning at Westminster, was delegated the task of preparing Edinburgh's reception, and his tremendous energies were devoted to ensuring that the occasion would not be forgotten in living memory. Chiefs and clansmen were summoned to appear in full regalia to pay their respects to the King. Processions, receptions and banquets were arranged and for two weeks Edinburgh was in festive mood. The King was delighted and proudly wore a kilt of Royal Stewart. The Assembly Room had its part to play, and two balls were held, one given by the Caledonian Hunt and the other by the Peers of Scotland. It is recorded that a throne hung with rich crimson velvet and surmounted by a canopy was placed at the east end of the ballroom. But the King did not occupy it, preferring to mingle with the company. Some idea of the grandeur of the scene can be obtained from the painting, ascribed to Turner, at present hung outside the room. In the words of *'The Scotsman'*, 'the function more than realised all previous conceptions of grandeur and magnificence.'

Sir Walter Scott again enters the scene when, at a Theatrical Fund Association function in the Assembly Room five years later, he publicly acknowledged that he was the author of The Waverley Novels. Dickens visited the room twice, on the second occasion reading his *'Christmas Carol'* to the Philosophical Institution. Thackeray's visit, however, in 1856, does not seem to have been quite so successful.   He was hissed down in one of his readings for making disparaging remarks about Mary, Queen of Scots.

In 1843 the Music Hall, with its ten-thousand-crystal chandelier was added to the rooms.   Edinburgh had then a social centre worthy of a capital city and the major role of the Assembly Room moved from being a place holding regular dances to that of a ballroom, catering for special functions.   The George Street Assembly Rooms have become a regular venue for regimental and other major balls, and a study of programmes will show that the functions held in these glittering surroundings give full support to our traditional dances.

SKYE JOURNEY

Then aye afore he socht his bed
He danced the Gillie Callum.
The Pawkie Duke — David Rorie (1867-1946)

In Portree, in the year 1878, eleven men, six bearing the name MacDonald, took the decision to establish an annual Skye Gathering. The objectives of the Gathering were simple and direct: by means of annual balls to encourage Highland dancing and the wearing of Highland dress. Membership was to be limited to fifty gentlemen of Skye or adjoining islands or of mainland proximity. The first members were obviously men of vigour, as, the decision having been taken, work commenced on the building of a Gathering Hall on ground behind the old prison in Portree and the first Skye Gathering Ball took place in 1879. Its programme was typical of the place and time — Eightsomes, Foursomes, Lancers and Quadrilles. The very traditionally inclined membership, which still stands at fifty today, has ensured that any changes are made gradually, and it has taken a number of years to see the inclusion and popularisation of *The Duke of Perth, Hamilton House, Reel of the 51st Division,* and now *Mairi's Wedding.*

The Skye Gathering Ball is a test of stamina. Attendance involves two successive nights' dancing from ten in the evening until six in the morning, with supper and breakfast providing much needed fortification. A twenty-dance programme with encores (frequently more than one) ensures busy feet. In pre-war days, catering was the responsibility of the members' families, when, with appropriately timed shoots, grouse pie and game pate figured prominently on the menu. Today, professional caterers have taken over. But nothing has been lost from the colour of the scene. Dress remains formal:

35

Highland dress, tails or uniforms for men; ladies on the first night wear sashes with plain long dresses usually dispensing with their sashes on the second night to adopt a patterned or multi-coloured gown.

The Centenary Ball in 1979 again showed the spirit of tradition which permeates the Skye Gathering. The hall, as usual, was decorated with heather, plaids and vases of rowan berries in brackets around the walls. Efforts were made to include the dances of the 1879 programme and the members' Thirty-twosome reel was still a major feature. Some of the musicians playing on the two nights could claim an association with the Ball going back nearly fifty years and the custom of providing an amateur band the opportunity to play during supper was maintained.

Some twenty miles to the north-west of Portree, across the waist of Skye, lies the castle of Dunvegan. There are larger, more handsome and more striking castles than Dunvegan, but none surely which exude so strongly a quality which can best be described as charisma. Dunvegan is at one with its surroundings, and its pull is irresistible.

Dunvegan has been the hereditary home of the MacLeods for centuries. Many readers will have some recollections of Dame Flora MacLeod who died in 1976 at the age of ninety-nine and who stamped her personality on a scene which stretched far from the Island of Skye. To her, kinship was paramount, and the MacLeods who visited Dunvegan every year from all parts of the world, or who attended the Clan Gatherings, were made aware that our social fabric would be all the poorer by the loosening of clan and family links.

Much has been written about the MacLeods and Dunvegan over hundreds of years. Any student of those writings cannot fail to notice the strong social theme in them. One translation from the Gaelic describes it admirably:

With Roderick Mor
MacLeod of Banners
In his great house
I have been joyful
Dancing merry
On a wide floor
the fiddle playing
to put me to sleep
The pipe playing
To wake me in the morning
Bear my greeting
To Dunvegan.

In more recent times social evenings seem to have been held in what is now the drawing room but was formerly the Great Hall. There, dancing to a fiddle and piano with the carpet in place was, in the words of one guest, a most peaceful and musical experience.

The great legend of Dunvegan with dancing connections, of course, concerns the Bratach Sith or Fairy Flag. The story goes that the birth of an heir was being celebrated in the castle, and the mother, attracted by the sounds of music and dancing in the hall, decided to leave her baby for a few minutes to view the activities. On entering the hall, however, she was whisked away to dance and left her offspring longer than she had intended. Suddenly remembering that the baby had been left only partly clothed, she rushed upstairs to the child's room. Opening the door, she heard music of unearthly sweetness and saw, gathered round the cot, a fairy choir. Wrapped around the young heir was a mystic banner. Astonished, she lifted up the baby and carried him, in his magic covering, down to the dancers in the hall below. As she entered the hall a fairy song was heard promising that, on three occasions, the flag, if waved aloft, would save the Chief and his clan in a time of peril. The fairy lullaby is still sung over babies belonging to the chiefly house who are born in the castle. And it is also recorded that the flag has twice been waved aloft in times of clan peril in war, with victory being achieved on both occasions. Today, the rather threadbare Fairy Flag may be seen in a glass-fronted display case in the drawing room of Dunvegan Castle. Regrettably the fairy voices have not yet been recorded.

There must be few people who do not automatically associate the name MacCrimmon with the playing of the pipes,. Just a few miles north of Dunvegan lies Borreraig, the ancestral home of the Mac-Crimmons who were the hereditary pipers to the MacLeod chiefs and whose playing has become legendary over the years. There, at Borreraig, the MacCrimmons established their piping collge and they are accepted as the first composers and teachers of the pibroch. Today, on the site, a unique museum tells the story of how the bagipe and its music developed.

Of all the MacCrimmon pipers, the greatest, according to Dr. I. F. Grant in *'The MacLeods: The History Of A Clan'*, was Patrick Mor MacCrimmon. And to Patrick Mor is attributed the rather touching lines said to have been composed on the death of Rory Mor, the rumbustious MacLeod chief:

Give me my pipes I'll home them carry,
In these sad halls I dare not tarry
My pipes hand o'er, my heart is sore
For Rory Mor, my Rory Mor

In 1746 an Act of Proscription forbade the playing of bagpipes in the Highlands. Up to that time, of course, the pipes had been the traditional instrument providing music for reels. While it is true that the Act of Proscription was not enforced for many years, the pipes nevertheless were removed from the scene at a time when country dancing was rapidly evolving and they were thus prevented from taking part in the evolutionary process. In later years the pattern at many functions was for pipes to be played for reels and fiddles for country dances. Not a very common practice today, which is something of a loss to dancers, especially if an Eightsome or Bonnie Anne be on the programme.

HOPETOUN HOUSE

One of the most natural instances of the effect of blank verse occurred to the late Earl of Hopetoun. His Lordship observed one of his shepherds poring in the fields upon Milton's 'Paradise Lost'; and having asked him what book it was, the man answered, 'An't please your Lordship , this is a very odd sort of an author; he would fain rhyme, but canna get at it.'
Boswell's Life of Johnson

Often described as Scotland's greatest Adam mansion, Hopetoun House stands in magnificent parkland overlooking the river Forth some mile and a half upstream of the river's famous bridges. The ancestral home of the Marquess of Linlithgow, Hopetoun has been occupied by the Hope family since the original house was built in 1703. That greatest of architects, William Adam, started to re-design and extend the house in 1721 and it is interesting to note that Hopetoun house is portrayed on Adam's tomb in Greyfriars Churchyard, Edinburgh — public recognition that it represents his greatest masterpiece.

Hopetoun, then, exudes elegance to a remarkable degree. John Mackay, who visited it in the eighteenth century, had his own way of portraying its extravagant lay-out:

This fine Palace and Garden lies in the middle of a spacious Park well stocked with Deer and environed with a Stone Wall. To the South of the Great Avenue lies the Kitchen Garden; and joining to it a House and Walk for Pheasants and Plantations for other Fowls and Beasts; and under the Earl's great Terrace is a Bed of Oysters from whence his kitchen is supplied all the Year round in the greatest quantities.

In due course much of the interior design work was to be carried out by Adam's talented sons. Today, the visitor to Hopetoun sees many

furnishings and hangings specially made for the various magnificent apartments well over two hundred years ago.

Of all the splendid occasions that have taken place at Hopetoun House the visit by King George IV in August 1822 must rank as the greatest. The West Lothian Cavalry and the Royal Artillery were on parade, and the Royal Company of Archers lined the stairs while the Scots Greys, with their strong West Lothian connection, were drawn up on the front lawn. His Majesty, we are told, lunched sparingly on turtle soup and three glasses of wine before knighting Henry Raeburn, the famous portrait painter.

Although dancing was a regular feature of the social life that took place in Hopetoun House in the eighteenth century, our interest must centre on the ballroom as it is used by dancers today. Originally an indoor riding school, it was transformed in the early years of the nineteenth century into one of the largest private ballrooms in Scotland. This great room, over a hundred feet in length, nearly thirty feet high and capable of taking four sets across, is remarkable for the glorious tapestries which almost clothe the walls. These tapestries illustrate the legend of Dido and Aeneas from the *Iliad*. Believed to be of Brussels' manufacture around the early years of the eighteenth century, the tapestries are in beautiful condition and their rich brown and deep blue hues provide a wonderful background to the dancing scene.

The ballroom of Hopetoun House, however, is not to be regarded as just a showpiece. Although it has been used for Prime Ministerial functions (it can seat four hundred for a meal), mannequin parades, antique fairs and so on, it provides the setting for many important dancing occasions. The Junior Highland Ball may be relatively new, but the Linlithgow and Stirlingshire Hunt and the Pony Club Balls are long-standing events. The ballroom, filled with around two hundred dancers, the men in Highland dress, indeed presents a quite magnificent sight, and it is no wonder that there is difficulty in obtaining tickets for such occasions as the St. Andrew's Night Ball organised for many years by Mrs. Mary Prentice. Mention must also be made of Marjorie Duffield's popular dance held in June in aid of the Hopetoun Trust, where attendance in the ballroom is usually preceded by open air dancing on the lawn. Miss Duffield is, of course, the deviser of the '*Hopetoun Suite of Dances*', the music for which was composed by Jack Stalker, and this leads on to an interesting discovery.

While it is almost a Scottish tradition for band leaders to come from country parts, it must be almost unique for an estate to boast of two bands. Yet such is the Hopetoun record. Jack Stalker's band has a fine reputation well beyond its locality. Indeed, Jack is one of the few band leaders to have completed a tour round Caledonian Societies in Africa. A solo fiddle player of distinction, he has performed before royalty, and adds composition to his talents. But a personal view of his great popularity is his unerring ability to fit the right tunes to a dance. The other band on the estate is Vic Laidlaw's Lothian Country Dance Band which plays at many important functions and has recorded with some success. The reader will readily understand why Hopetoun House occupies such a prominent position in country dancing circles.

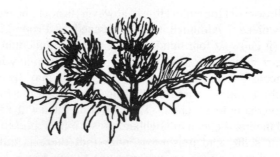

THE HIGHLANDERS' INSTITUTE, GLASGOW

Afore we end, strike up the spring
O' Thulican and Hieland fling
County Meeting — Lady Nairne (1766—1845)

In his splendidly readable autobiography, the late John (Lord) Bannerman relates how his great-grandfather settled in Glasgow. The forebear was returning home to the Strath of Kildonan with twelve grapeshot wounds in his body after the battle of Waterloo. On reaching Glasgow he was told he need go no further. The family croft was no more: the family had been evicted.

There were many Highlanders such as Bannerman putting down their roots in Glasgow in the early, middle and latter years of the nineteenth century. While the Clearances forced many to seek the shores of Canada and America (to the great benefit of those countries), the apparent security of a Clydeside trembling under the impetus of an industrial revolution drew its share to its bosom. The growing slums of Glasgow replaced the hillside crofts as the homes of the Gael. Lack of land, lack of job opportunities and shortages of food in the Highlands and Islands ensured that the momentum of the drift to Glasgow was maintained over many years.

While the Highlander is more than capable of being a cosmopolitan figure, it is easy to understand why in those Glasgow days he so eagerly sought the company of his fellows. The link of the Gael with his past is strong and the change from hillside to factory floor or city street must strongly have fanned his natural inclination to keep his past with him. There was no way the songs, dances and music of the Highlands and Islands were to be forgotten: no way the stories and poems were to be jettisoned. Especially, there was no way the Gaelic tongue was to be forgotten, and as front doors closed at night on busy streets there was an easy and welcome slipping back to the native language. It was inevitable, therefore, that social and other centres for the Gael would be formed. Gaelic churches were established and even some English-language churches introduced Gaelic services. Clan associations were set up, as were local societies, and these continue to thrive to the present day.

Over the years there was a natural movement to seek the establishment of a focal point for Gaelic culture in Glasgow. In 1780 the Glasgow Gaelic Club was formed and for the following decade met in various taverns and hotels in Glasgow. The Club's first ball is recorded as having taken place in 1792 after which it became a fairly regular event. Strenuous affairs these balls must have been, starting at 7 p.m. with a Reel of Tullochgorum, and continuing, with a break for a meal at midnight, until dawn. But support for the Club for some reason or another dwindled and 1841 saw the last ball taking place.

While the Clan and Island and various Highland Societies continued to flourish, the need for a common focal point continued to be felt and in 1890 the *Ceilidh Nan Gaidheal,* The Highlanders' Ceilidh, was founded, meeting in the Gael Lodge of the Freemasons in West Regent Street. Around that time, too, the High School Ceilidh was formed, which was, in due course, to patronise the Highlanders' Institute.

In 1925 the Highlanders' Institute opened its doors in Elmbank Street. During its thirty odd years of life it was to become the meeting place *par excellence* for the Gaels and their friends. A place of tremendous atmosphere, it bubbled with a level of activity that it is hard now to visualise. Dancing took place every night of the week beginning on a Monday night, according to one former Master of Ceremonies, with fairly genteel dancing and warming up every night to Friday evening when full-blooded exercise was the order. Saturday was the climax of the week for the Instutute. Then, three hundred dancers might be on the floor in the dance hall while in the gymnasium the Pipers' Association would ensure that all who were willing to play would be given the opportunity. Add to this various ceilidhs in the upstairs rooms and one can understand the affection that developed for this old building. The Institute was a place for the whole family with youngsters to grandfathers enjoying their native culture.

Such support ensured a financially sound meeting place, and regular use of the Institute was ensured through the affiliation of various associations such as the Lewis and Harris, Skye, Tiree, Badenoch, Wester Ross as well as the Clan Donald, MacLean, Cameron, and so on.

The Institute moved to premises in Berkley Street in 1961. It was not to prove a fruitful move. Perhaps the location was wrong. Perhaps the new building was just incapable of maintaining the exciting and yet authentic atmosphere of the Elmbank Street premises. The dropping population of Glasgow as people moved to the new towns of East Kilbride and Cumbernauld was another contributory factor to falling attendances. A policy of letting rooms to outside organisations was introduced in an attempt to maintain viability and a licensed bar was opened. Such moves had little effect and the door closed on a way of life that had become a social anchor to so many.

Today the clan gatherings and Island and Highland associations still meet. Following the closure of the Institute at Berkley Street, the old St. Andrew's Hall became a favoured venue for their social events. When it was burned down, the associations transferred their allegiance to the City Halls. Yet when one considers how the Highlanders have maintained their dances and social culture over the years in Glasgow, one finds it hard to believe that a Pheonix will not rise again from the ashes. The Institute or something similar may again grace the scene.

GLENS OF ANGUS

My daddie was a fiddler fine,
My minnie she made mantie, O;
And I mysel' a thumpin' quine,
And danc'd the reel o' stumpie, O.
The Reel O' Stumpie — Robert Burns (1759—1796)

Angus is one of the least known counties in Scotland. The traveller on his north or south route will likely hold to the coast road or journey through the valley of Strathmore and miss the glens. Although noting the background hills it is unlikely he will seek to penetrate the hinterland. The Angus glens all come to abrupt ends, and there is a natural reluctance to explore an unknown part of the country that does not provide a circular route. This is to be regretted as the Angus Glens with names like Clova, Isla, Prosen and Lethnot provide some of the finest scenery in Scotland.

But if the traveller will take the Edzell road from Brechin he is on his way to finding one of the most unusual dancing places in Scotland. The hamlet of Tarfside is some fifteen miles up the Glen Esk road from Edzell, in the heart of the hills. Truly, it qualifies for the description 'remote'.

The Masonic Hall in Tarfside is an old, somewhat dreary and even ugly building. Its dull exterior gives no hint of the gaiety it contains a number of times a year when the keepers, stalkers, shepherds and hill farmers gather to dance with a vigour seldom seen in town or city dancing assemblies. Here, dancing pumps are unknown, and working brogues are the order of dress. One is left in no doubt that dancing is essentially a masculine activity.

The dances at 'Tarfie' are part of life in the glen. There is the Farmers' Dance, the dance after the sheep-dog trials, dances in the Summer to provide a change of exercise for the young people enjoying

46

Tarfside, Glenesk, in the 1920's. *Photo: Glenesk Folk Museum.*

working holidays as beaters and, above all in importance, the Masons' Ball, when the night's dancing is traditionally preceded by the consumption of monstrous helpings of venison pie.

Tarfside dances deserve a mention in this chronicle because they represent such an unusual contribution to the dancing scene. The Lancers and Quadrilles are still danced by people who have been brought up with them. Above all, this is 'birling' country, with the enjoyment of the night being assessed by the amount of sweat exuded. Broun's Reel follows an Eightsome and Strip the Willow with a Schottische offering the opportunity to regain breath.

In the absence of a formal programme repetition is accepted as the norm. One lady encountered claimed that the best night she had ever had at Tarfie included four Broun's Reels and two Lancers. Tarfie dances seem to last for hours, but then they do not finish on the day they started! Billed for an eight o'clock start, they will not be properly under way until ten, with the finishing time determined more by the physical condition of the dancers than the desire of the band to make a forty or perhaps more miles journey home to their beds. Yet however exhilarating and wonderful a night at Tarfie may be there is a sadness as one considers the future. The Glen is slowly losing its people. The young beaters and holiday makers who swell the numbers dancing during the Summer months have not learned many country dances on their home territories, and have to be weaned on to them. The natural good manners of the Glen folk encourage them to restrict the range of dances at their functions to help the visitors to enjoy themselves. Yet there is ground for optimism too. The remaining young people in the Glen still show a marked preference for the country dances. And who knows how many visitors have their enthusiasm so fired by experiencing Tarfie dancing that they pursue these country dances when they return to their more sophisticated home surroundings.

Lethnot, the next glen, has little regular dancing, the population tending to journey to Edzell for their fun and relaxation, but the

'The Lancers' at Glenesk.   The young people of the Glen grew up in a dancing environment.   *Photo: Mrs. Jock Mitchell, Glenesk, Angus.*

Cortachy Hall at the foot of Glen Clova and the nearby hotel comfortably cater for the the needs of that glen. Various rural associations run dances throughout the year at the Cortachy Hall, while the dance after the games is still an event of some prominence. The country dances still feature strongly at local weddings with the inevitable Broun's Reels, Eightsomes, Strip the Willows and Lancers forming the bulk of the programme.

Glen Prosen has suffered badly from depopulation and dances at the Prosen Hall have faded over the past two or three years. Glen Prosen, of course, is remembered for its association with Captain Scott, who was a frequent visitor to the glen. Here he planned his famous journey to the South Pole, and an exhibition is maintained in his cottage.

In Glen Isla, though, the picture is much brighter, with a number of well-organised dances being run throughout the winter months. The main summer function, of course, is the dance held after the Glen Isla games. The interest of the Glen Isla people in their social activities has not always met with approval. In the *Montrose Advertiser and Brechin Review* of September 6th, 1850, a gentleman signing himself *Abillino* did not pull his punches.

> *The hall erected for the ball of the gathering has cost five if not ten times more than the barn-like kirks of Prosen and Clova. The hall occupies the foreground and the church the back. The comparison between money spent on religion and intellectual improvement of the people and what is swallowed up by this frivolous and degrading gathering and its ball rouses indignation.*

Remembering that at the time the hall was built the glen was without a library and the school was open only for a few months every year, one has to admit that the Isla folk must have been enthusiastic dancers, and that perhaps *Abillino* had a point.

It is worth mentioning that only four miles from Isla, albeit in Perthshire, an hotel runs a country dance every Saturday night with visitors travelling up to thirty miles to enjoy themselves.

Angus and its neighbouring counties have long been famous for the quality of their country dance bands.   Looking back over the years one thinks of such names as the Hawthorn Band, Ian Powrie, Jim and Will Cameron and the legendary Jimmy Shand.   What great days they were, and what great nights!

PEEBLES WAY

With that Will Swane came sweatand out,
Ane meikle miller man;
'Gif I sall dance have done, lat see
Blaw up the bagpipe than!
The schamous dance I maun begin;
I trow it sall not pane.'
So heavily he hochit about
To see him, Lord, as they ran,
That tide, Of Peblis to the play.
Peblis to the Play — Anon. (circa. 15th century)

The Tontine Hotel is situated half way down the High Street of Peebles.   Set slightly back from the main road, it presents a square, squat exterior.   It is very ordinary, the kind of building that may be seen in many parts of the country.   Its story, however, is somewhat unusual and here we must move first from dancing to another form of exercise.

The Tweedale Shooting Club, the oldest such club in the country, was formed at Peebles in 1790.   A few years later some of its members decided to build an hotel and ballroom in the town, and to do it under the 'Tontine' principle, one which is quite illegal today.   It involved investment in a project by a number of people who, according to the success of the venture, would each receive an annual dividend, and who owned the building jointly.   As members of the original group died off, the group of owners got smaller and smaller, and eventually the actual ownership of the property was vested in the last member of the consortium left alive.   This method of establishing new enterprises was for many years not uncommon in Scotland, but abuse of the system, or, should it be said, the number of unexplained deaths which followed in the wake of such enterprises, led to the Tontine Principle being outlawed early in the nineteenth century.

Dancing at Traquair House, near Peebles.
Photo: Miss Dorothy Leurs, Edinburgh.

However, the diehards from the Shooting Club completed their hotel and ballroom in 1808 and since then the ballroom has been a regular rendezvous for the Club on their dancing occasions. The ballroom is an impressive room built in the style of Adam, with bay windows and a minstrels' gallery. Traditionally decorated with white woodwork and in pastel shades, it retains the original fireplace and some furniture of the same age. The first chandeliers have had to be replaced by ones of a later date, but the room, frequently used for dining purposes, warrants in every way its use for official functions by Peebles Town Council. There is evidence to suggest that French prisoners from the Napoleonic Wars worked on the building and that a number of French officers were lodged in the Tontine whilst on parole in 1811-1815.

The oldest inhabited house in Scotland, Traquair, lies about eight miles east of Peebles. Traquair is steeped in history and in an unbroken line has housed the Stuart family for ten centuries. Perhaps its most interesting legend is that of the famous Bear gates at the entrance to the house which were closed by order of the fifth Earl of Traquair after Prince Charles Edward Stuart passed through them in 1745, with the vow that they would not be opened again until a Stuart once again sat on the throne.

> *Dool an' Sorrow fa'en Traquair*
> *An' the Getts that wer shut at Charlie's comin'*
> *He vowed wad be opened nevermair*
> *Till a Stuart King was crooned in Lunnon.*

Fortunately for those interested in the dancing scene at least, some members of the family were compulsive diary keepers and thus we have access to records which display the importance of country dances to this old Scottish family. In 1773 one Mary Ravenscroft became the wife of the seventh Earl of Traquair. The following year a daughter, Louisa, was born, and from the year 1782 onwards there are regular diary entries telling of the daughter's progress with Mr. Harper, her dancing master. Mr. Harper, it seems, was an important

acquaintance of the family, and after Louisa's lessons he would stay in the house to join the family dancing later in the evening in the drawing room.   Should his presence be required elsewhere, the fiddler would remain behind to provide the dance music.   The fiddler, indeed, seems to have been on regular stand-by, as on dreich days he would be brought into the house to cheer up the company.

The Town House at Peebles appears to have been a regular venue for balls towards the end of the eighteenth century, and one 1782 entry from the Traquair diaries gives a graphic description of what a well dressed young lady might wear: *'Dress for Ball was a corded dimity scarcastern with one row of trimming of chirton round ye skirt tied at ye hands with pink ribbon satin belt worked with beads.   Bow of white ribbon behind ye left side of the head.   Dark scarlet silk shoes.'*   The diaries appear to draw a distinction betwen dances and country dances, possibly to differentiate between the continental introductions of that time and Scottish reels.   The dancing of hornpipes is regularly mentioned and Blackamore's Jig appears to have been a favourite.

An interesting insight into the relationship between the laird's family and their staff is also contained within the diaries. On 31st January 1784, the family appears to have had a particularly fine meal with a goodly supply of claret before following Lady Traquair to the great dining room for country dancing. The group was joined later by the servants and dancing continued until four in the morning. The following day's entry is even more revealing: '*Cook was let blood in ye evening for pain in her side, she had got dancing too much the night before.*

Dancing in Traquair House continued well into the present century as a form of home entertainment. The estate people were not forgotten, and the malt loft with its splendid floor was frequently used for dances by the estate workers.

THE LONACH HIGHLAND BALL

*Nowhere beats the heart so kindly as beneath
the tartan plaid.*

William Edmondstoun Ayton (1813—1865) writing about Charles
Edward at Versailles

In 1823, Sir Charles Forbes, Baronet of Newe and Edinglassie in
Strathdon, founded the Lonach Highland and Friendly Society to
commemorate the coming of age of his son. The objects of the
Society give an insight into what were considered priorities by a
leading figure possessed of a social conscience at that time. They
were:

*To preserve Highland dress and the Gaelic language.
To support loyal, peaceable and manly conduct, and
To promote social and benevolent feelings amongst the
inhabitants of the district.*

Little could the noble laird have realised at that time how many ripples
would issue from his simple wish to help the people in Strathdon.

The Society performed solely in the field of benevolence until an
annual Games was introduced in 1836. The now famous march of
the Lonach Highlanders, which had its origins as a church parade,
also started at that time. One form of exercise leads to another, and
it was not long before a Games Dance was introduced and 1845 saw
the building of a hall (next to the ruin of Colquhonnie Castle) where
dancing could take place and which, in addition, provided a social
gathering place for the people of Strathdon. The years 1850-1861
saw the Lonach men carrying out three-day marches to Braemar and
back to take part in the games there and to be reviewed by Queen
Victoria. These marathon marches increased public interest in the
Lonach scene and the growing interest and attendances encouraged
the extension of the hall to provide ballroom facilities in 1900. It is

57

The Lonach men, with their patron Col. Sir John Forbes, enjoy a traditional dram while on the march.

Photo: Gibbie McIntosh, Strathdon.

not exactly recollected just when the decision was taken to add the Lonach Ball as a separate social occasion to the Strathdon Games dance, but it was probably in the early years of this century.   Certainly looking back over the years, in 1938, Charles Christie in his *'Stray Memories of Strathdon'* recalls that the principal events of the year were the Conversazione and the Lonach Ball.

The former event, perhaps sadly, no longer exists.   Apparently the young ladies delegated to head a table and entertain guests did not like being surpassed by their neighbours, and vied with each other in the nature of table decorations and the quality of their silverware. Competition between them ultimately reached such proportions that a halt had to be called.

The two social events today, then, are the Games Dance, followed a week later by the Highland Ball.   How much dancing takes place at the Games Dance can be left to the imagination.   Some years, over eight hundred people have bought tickets.   But the Ball, with restricted numbers, has all the colour of a truly grand Highland affair.   The beams in the hall are swathed with tartan and the *de rigeur* stags' heads are complemented by trophies from safaris made by members of the Forbes family.   Nor should one miss the paintings depicting the famous marches of the Lonach men to Braemar, where, after sleeping out, a full-scale breakfast would be consumed at linen-covered tables in the open air.

The dance programme for the Ball is worthy of attention.   According to Gibbie McIntosh, the energetic and unbelievably committed Secretary to the Society, the same programme has been followed every year since the War, with but the one change that the Grand March now leads into an Eightsome instead of a Foursome reel. The Programme reads:

Grand March	Gay Gordons	Dashing White Sergeant
Eightsome Reel	Modern Waltz	Military Two-Step
Old-time Waltz	One Step	Petronella
Polka	Old-Time Waltz	Quick Step

St. Bernard's Waltz
Eightsome Reel
Fox Trot
Polka
Gay Gordons

Quadrilles
St. Bernard's Waltz
Old-Time Waltz
Strip The Willow
Boston Two-Step

Waltz

Sadly, and unexpectedly in a Glen so near to Speyside, there is not a Strathspey on the programme. The Quadrille is regarded as a Strathdon favourite and there is music in existence, unfortunately undated, of *The Lonach Highland Quadrille* arranged by Helen, Lady Forbes.

Perhaps the Society has not attained all its objectives in that little Gaelic is now evident in Strathdon. But the enthusiastic response over the years to Games, Gathering, Dance and the Highland Ball is a fond tribute to one man's initiative.

60

JIM McLEOD AT DUNBLANE HYDRO

'Weel done,' quoth he: 'Play up,' quoth she
'weel bobb'd' quoth Rob the Ranter
'Tis worth my while to play indeed,
When I hae sic a dancer.'
Maggie Lauder — Anonymous

Dunblane Hydro stands majestically on a knoll some five hundred feet above sea level midst twenty acres of wooded garden. The fourth largest hotel in Scotland, a first glance takes in a building that suggests Italian architecture unexpectedly harmonising with the slightly Highland atmosphere of Dunblane. Not a natural home for country dancing, one might think. Yet for over twenty years the name of Dunblane Hydro has been almost synonymous to many with the name of a band that has done much more than its share to promote country dancing and popularise music so essentially Scottish.

Jim McLeod is a local man whose roots are strong in the area. Raised in an age when children were expected to learn how to make their own entertainment as a qualification for later years, he learned to play the piano. Thoughts of ultimately earning his livelihood as a professional musician did not enter his head, although as he matured the idea developed of playing part-time as a satisfying hobby. But even at that stage there was developing within him the aspiration to be the focal point of the entertainment and not merely the background melody maker. It is an attitude which has coloured his whole approach to his career and was to lead in due course to his long association with the Hydro and the worlds of stage and broadcasting.

National Service in the Royal Air Force provided Jim McLeod with the opportunity to play regularly in a dance band. Shortly after demobilisation he adopted the life -style of the semi-professional musician, playing in the evenings at the Forest Hills Hotel, Aberfoyle. His approach to the BBC for an audition was successful.

His first broadcasts, though, were far from what was anticipated, the only spot found for his band being in Children's Hour. But it was a start leading on to an afternoon's programme, again for children, 'Doon on the Mains', a farm story which it must be admitted offered little opportunity to the band to display its talents. However the McLeod foot was in the B.B.C. door and it was not long before the opportunity for Jim McLeod to put out his distinctive brand of country dance music over the air presented itself. He was on his way.

In any successful career there is usually at least one moment of fate. To Jim McLeod it came in the year 1962. Reo Stakis, the well-known Scottish restaurateur, had bought Dunblane Hydro. The Palm Court atmosphere which had welcomed thousands of visitors taking the nearby spa waters over the years departed as Stakis invited McLeod to provide the Hydro's music. It was an offer not to be refused. The Hydro provided the environment in which he wanted to work, while his respect for the talented restaurateur provided the basis for a long and happy relationship. About this time McLeod cut his first disc. This was on Parlophone Records with the association of George Martin, who was later to produce the Beatles' albums. McLeod in due course switched to Decca, record-ing either in the Hydro or in London, before ultimately producing his own tapes.

However, the programme which brought the name of Jim McLeod to the fore was the radio series 'On Tour.' For thirteen years McLeod and his band covered the country from the Shetlands to the Borders broadcasting weekly for twelve weeks every year. Broad-casts went out from all sorts of places, from school and village halls to castles like Dunvegan. Listeners loved the swing of his music, audiences warmed to the sincerity of his efforts to produce a 'That was a grand night' feeling. The move from radio to television was natural, and for seven years the band appeared regularly on 'The Kilt Is My Delight.' "Appeared" is probably not the best word to use, for in the first programmes the cameras focussed on the dancers and singers completely ignoring the band.   The accepted suggestion to feature the band in a request spot brought such an avalanche of letters that from there on there was little doubt about whom the public wanted to see on the screen.   To crown this success, Jim McLeod was presented with the Grampian Personality of the Year Award in 1979.   Television success led Jim McLeod to present his own band show in theatres and for many years his annual show in Her Majesty's Theatre, Aberdeen has played to capacity audiences.

The success of the McLeod band as entertainers must never detract from the contribution Jim McLeod had made to Scottish Country dancing.   He is regularly in demand for major functions and there are few great dancing events in Scotland or England that he has not played at.   The weekly country dances at Dunblane Hydro during the Summer months are highly successful as are the dance week-ends held in various places.   The broadcasting of country dance music is still important to Jim McLeod although he has now moved up-market to Radio 2.   Radio Clyde occasionally uses the soft voice as a presenter of a successful record programme.   It seems that Jim McLeod cannot help making contact with his public.   He is the entertainer par excellence.

JUST OVER THE BORDER

It was determinit there suld be na familiaritie betwix Scottis men and Inglis men, nor marriage to be contrakit betwix them, nor conventions on holydais at gammis and plays, nor merchandres to be maid amang them....Bot that statutis and artiklis are adnullit, for ther hes been grit familiaritie, and conventions, and makyng of merchandreis, on the boirdours, this lang tyme betwix Inglis men and Scottis men.

The Complaynt of Scotland (1549) — Sir David Lyndsay (1490-1555)

As a quick scan through the Royal Scottish Country Dance Society Year Book will show, Scottish country dancing can be found throughout the world. This is hardly surprising. The Scot is a natural traveller, willing to put down his roots or take work anywhere in the world. And when he does, then inevitably he becomes more Scottish in cultural terms than he was when domiciled amongst his own folk. Burns and haggis, St. Andrew's Night and country dancing become woven into the fabric of his social life. It is his peculiar way of retaining contact with his native land.

This study, however, confines itself to the influence and position of Scottish country dancing 'just over the Border', in those northern English counties which over the centuries had a war/peace relationship with Scotland. The people from either side of the Border have much in common. They are hardy, independant people whose leisure pursuits are strong in physical activity. Hunting, shooting, rugby and hill-walking figure high in popularity. It is easy to understand a liking for a form of dancing that requires effort and activity. While today the Border can be regarded as a fixture, it has to be remembered that it was not always so, although the River Tweed does offer a natural barrier. Particularly in the east, the position of the Border would fluctuate according to the fortunes of war and the holding of land on both sides of the Border was not uncommon. George

MacDonald Fraser in his '*Steel Bonnets*' points out that at one time the extreme punishment was death for a Scotsman marrying an English girl without the permission of the appropriate March Warden. But love will always find a way, and the wenching rose to such a degree that, as the '*Complaynt of Scotland*' points out, all such restrictions had to be anulled. The intermarriage that followed resulted in families of the same name being found on both sides of the Border: Armstrongs, Grahams,and Bells being obvious examples.

As well as marriage bonds being formed, trade and social occasions such as horse racing meetings brought the two sides together socially. It is not difficult to understand, then, how an appreciation of Scottish dances could grow and influence the North of England dances. The pipes, too, were found south of the Border, and few people today are aware that Newcastle still boasts a bagpipe museum. All this points to the nearness to the truth of the Geordie's boast that he is a Scotsman with brains!

In the passage of time the dancing link was to be strengthened by the Scottish 'dancies' who crossed the border to teach. Scottish-type dances would be composed by the 'dancies' but given English names in honour of their patron. English steps found their way into Scottish dances such as the *Northumbrian Rant* step in *Strip the Willow* and the *Gay Gordons*. *Corn Rigs* was given a distinct variation and some tunes like Hill's *High Level Hornpipe* moved North. Evolution and integration march side by side.

Today when one looks at Scottish country dancing in Cumberland and Northumberland, it is necessary to approach the subject from two angles. First there is the assessment to be made of the strength of country dance clubs; second, a look is required at how popular the Scottish dances are in the world of folk dancing catered to by the ceilidh bands currently enjoying increasing popularity.

There are now over a dozen Scottish country dance clubs in Northumberland and Cumberland holding membership with the Royal Scottish Country Dance Society. The largest, of course, is in

Newcastle, with nearly two hundred and fifty individual members. It is a thriving club and its ability to attract so many young people to its special children's dances bodes well for the future. While many North of England musicians are no mean players of Scottish country dance music, one must envy the association the Newcastle Branch has built up over the years with some of the finest players ever to grace the scene: Shand, Fitchet, Powrie, Johnstone and Rankine have all made their mark with the club and the *Newcastle Collection of Country Dance Tunes,* published in 1971 to commemorate the club's twenty-first birthday, contains an outstanding collection of compositions by these musical giants. Mention must be made, too, of Jack Armstrong, Piper to the Duke of Northumberland, who, exchanging his pipes for the fiddle, led the Barnstormers to a prominent position in the traditional music and dance fields.

But outwith the Tyneside metropolis, in places like Seahouses, Morpeth and Hexham, enthusiasm runs high. Here again the Scottish bands have made a distinct contribution. Jimmy Shand for many years regularly toured Northumbrian villages, naming many tunes after local people. Andrew Rankine, of course, resided in Whitley Bay for many years and was a great favourite at barn dances as well as at more formal functions.

Carlisle, too, is a pleasant mecca for country dancers, and many Scottish bands are prepared to travel to functions all over Cumbria. Many clubs operate outwith the R.S.C.D.S. circle, and country dancing is a favourite pursuit at evening classes in many of the less populated places.

There is no popular movement in Scotland comparable to the folk dancing to ceilidh bands in the north of England. While the word '*ceilidh*' may have been borrowed, the English ceilidh consists mainly of dancing, although a song and recitation are often included. The guitar may feature in the ceilidh band, but essentially it plays folk music without the strident beat of the Scottish country dance band, so essential, of course, for precision dancing. Ignoring the actual dances themselves, for the moment, a number of differences can be highlighted between North of England ceilidh band dancing and Scottish country dancing. Firstly, there is a caller, who will carry responsibility for walking the dances through and giving guidance where necessary during the dances. Secondly, there is the expected lack of tartan, with dress stretching from 'come as you are' to black breeches and white stockings. There is an equal number of the sexes, and, if a subjective assessment is correct, a younger dancing population.

How, then, are Scottish dances faring in the world of the ceilidh band? Such bands regard the world as their oyster and draw on dances not only from the northern but from more southern parts; they introduce continental novelties and by no means neglect American folk dances. One enthusiast encountered claimed that many of the dances being imported from America were derived from dances originally exported from this country and were being received back in a more acceptable form. Certainly many of the progressions in American folk dances correspond with our own, the main differences being in techniques and the avoidance of dancing on the toes. The Scottish country dancer attending a ceilidh band function will find himself at home with the *Dashing White Sergeant, Strip the Willow* and the ubiquitous *Gay Gordons*, but may have to be satisfied with that little lot. He will, however, be pleased to hear many of his own tunes providing the music for English dances from Yorkshire upwards. Equally, he will be able to comment that some of the dances he sees possess a basic structure not so far removed from some of his own.

The ceilidh bands are making a tremendous contribution to the country dancing scene. Perhaps, due to evolution, they will prompt dancers to turn their attention to the Scottish dances which require, it is fair to say, in many cases, more concentration and application and thus provide a greater sense of achievement. If they do, the prospect is exciting; if they do not, no one can deny the pleasure they are giving to many who just want to spend a happy evening dancing.

ROBBIE SHEPHERD,
THE DUNECHT LOON

So here's to Strip the Willow, the polka and the reel,
Here's to country dances, the lancers and quadrille;
What's the use o' jazz for folk that's fed on brose and meal?
Sae pit a bit o' pith in't lads, wi' a' yer soul an' heel.
The Conversazione — Willie Kemp (from Kerr's 'Cornkisters')

In an age when radio and television feast largely on new material to retain listeners' and viewers' interest, any series that can boast a life of almost forty years, while fundamentally based on the same formula, obviously stands out as something unusual, if not verging on the unique. Programmes of Scottish country dance music were being broadcast on radio regularly certainly as long ago as 1946 and still today many tens of thousands tune in, with relish and unfailing regularity every Saturday evening, to B.B.C. Scotland for the enjoyment of "Take the Floor". Quite simply, it is a programme of Scottish country dance music with news of coming dances, followed by news of the activities of various Accordion and Fiddle Clubs. On the face of it, not a recipe for an outstanding radio show, but, as its adherents will avow, "Take The Floor" is not a superficial present-ation. It is a production that commands affection because it gets so close to the true feel and spirit of Scottish country dance music. It is an outstanding example of broadcasting professionalism being wedded to the simple things which ordinary people consider important. Such a marriage demands a catalytic character. The country dance scene and the programme have found one in Robbie Shepherd.

The village of Dunecht lies about twelve miles west of Aberdeen, in the direction of Strathdon. It is situated in the old "farm toun" area of the North-east, strong in folk-lore, cradle of the bothy ballads and habitat of a people to whom enjoyment is synonymous with music and dancing. In this environment Robbie Shepherd grew up. His teenage recollections show how much traditional music was part of his life — his father's excursions to Aberdeen to buy the latest Adam Rennie or Jim Cameron record; lying awake at nights listening to the music throbbing from the dances in the village hall just two doors down the street.   There was never any doubt that music was to be more than a transitory interest.

The hinterland of Aberdeen has produced perhaps more than its fair share of professional men, and it was a natural progression for young Robbie to train as an accountant.   From hard nights at evening classes and wide experience in industry, he set up his own practice in Aberdeen, which he still runs today.   But the music of his country had a grip on his soul, and shortly after leaving school, his love of comedy and Scottish songs was to take him into the Garlogie Four, a group which specialised in bothy ballads and became 'weel kent' faces at socials and weddings.   The group's entertainment value was such that it was, in due course, to obtain bookings at such places as the Tivoli theatre in Aberdeen, giving the Dunecht Loon the opportunity to meet the prominent band leaders of the 'fifties, when Scottish country dance music was enjoying its peak of popularity. Soon he was to take the short but significant step to developing his own spot in shows as character-comedy artist, looking strongly to his idol, Harry Gordon, the great Scots comedian, for inspiration.   Leaving the Garlogie Four, he found an increasing number of engagements open to him as a couthy country entertainer and compere of shows.   Whilst from then on, it was as a compere and evangelist of country music that he was to achieve his national standing, his own performance as an artiste should not be forgotten.   He is much in demand on the 'folk' scene, with his distinctive North-east voice particularly pleasing,in the mould of Willie Kemp and George S. Morris.

For ten years, during the 'sixties, Robbie Shepherd compered the biennial visits of the renowned Gallowglass Ceilidh Band, led by Pat McGarr, from Naas, near Dublin, to the Aberdeen and Angus area. At a time when country dance music was losing its popularity the band played to capacity audiences and incidentally, when sharing the bill with Jim Cameron's Band, performed to an audience of three thousand in the town hall of Cork, which sounds quite impressive until, one discovers that Jimmy Shand once played to ten thousand people at an open-air concert in the Union Terrace Gardens in Aberdeen. The increasing demand for his services as a compere now saw Robbie Shepherd attend nearly all the major Scottish musical occasiona, and his connection with the Braemar Highland Gathering started, where, for ten years now, crowds of thirty thousand have enjoyed his almost unique mixture of warmth and wit, coupled with the ability to provide the right comment for the moment.

To the delight of the population in the North-east, the B.B.C. opened Radio Aberdeen in the mid-seventies, and Robbie Shepherd accepted the invitation to introduce a programme of Scottish requests. The series was a success, and was followed by a further series where Robbie took the opportunity to look more seriously at Scottish traditional music, reminding his listeners of the contribution made to our musical culture by Shetland and Cape Breton fiddlers and many local musicians. He was involved in 'Take The Floor' from its earliest days and through this programme has extended his range of enthusiastic followers throughout the country.

Any discourse on Robbie Shepherd, of course, is incomplete if it does not recognise that anyone with his positive personality will be surrounded by some controversy. Two charges are laid at his door. Firstly, that as a national broadcasting figure he still presents himself as the simple Dunecht Loon instead of projecting a more up-market image, and secondly in a weekly programme, ostensibly for country dance enthusiasts, he devotes overmuch attention to Accordion and Fiddle Clubs. These points are of such basic importance to Robbie Shepherd himself that they warrant pursuance. Shepherd is, of course, a genuine product of the Aberdeenshire countryside. To him, country dancing is associated with the enjoyment of communities in village and town halls. Whilst never slow to praise, or indeed enthuse over, the magnificence of Scottish country dancing when performed with all the graciousness it is capable of receiving, he sees the priority as getting the masses to return to it for the sheer enjoyment it offers. He is on an evangelical crusade and considers it would be false to that crusade if he were to portray himself as being other than he is at heart.

A generation ago, a great broadcasting personality by the name of Wilfred Pickles raised eyebrows by adhering to his North of England accent when reading the news and hosting a number of quiz-type programmes, but his integrity and professionalism won him national affection at the end of the day. Robbie Shepherd is in the same mould. His views on Accordion and Fiddle Clubs are interesting. It must be remembered that as interest in Scottish country dancing faded in the 'sixties there was a compensating rise in listening to folk music in all its forms. Starting in the Borders and moving northwards, Accordion and Fiddle Clubs were formed, until today there are few places without at least one such club. Shepherd sees such clubs, along with country dance clubs and Strathspey and Reel societies, as part of one national movement concerned with the national folk culture of Scotland. He believes Accordion and Fiddle Clubs give up-and-coming musicians the opportunity to perform in public, which these enthusiasts would not otherwise get. In due course country dancing gains by the increasing number of musicians eager and competent to play in dance bands.

Today there is increased attention being paid to Scottish country dancing and its music. The Dunecht Loon has done more than his bit to stimulate that interest. Long may we be able to 'Take The Floor' on Saturday evenings!

THE DANCERS OF DON

> To dance thir damosellis them dicht,
> thir lasses licht of laitis
> their glovis was of the raffel richt,
> their schoon was of the straitis.

Christis Kirk of the Green — attributed variously to James I and James V.

Although it is over a quarter of a century since the Dancers of Don last graced the scene, the reputation of this remarkable group of dancers lingers on, and certainly in the North-east of Scotland there are many who ascribe legendary qualities to them. The dancing world has seen many outstanding demonstration and competition teams, yet it is certain that none have made such a mark on the community as the Dancers of Don. Not only did they give public enjoyment, they created public interest in country dancing.

The Dancers of Don, who mostly lived on Donside, were formed in 1933, meeting first of all in Fintray House near Dyce, Aberdeenshire. Their purpose primarily was to compete in the Country Dancing sections at the Music Festivals which, large or small, were, and indeed still are, to be found spread over the the North of Scotland. Certainly the group was formed from good dancers who were drilled assiduously. Even so, their climb to the top can only be described as phenomenal.

The Dancers of Don, however, were determined to take country dancing to a larger audience and, as their popularity grew they accepted the increasing number of invitations to demonstrate at functions stretching from Dundee to Inverness, while, in 1935, only two years after their inception, they demonstrated at the Manx Highland Gathering in Douglas, Isle of Man. The Dancers' first visit to London was in 1937, when they joined forces with the London

Gaelic Choir at the Cambridge Theatre. In following years they were to repeat their London success at the Cambridge Theatre, again in company with the London Gaelic Choir, who at that time boasted two fine Gold Medal Mod winners in Robert King and James McPhee. The night's programme would be built, of course, around set dances, but Highland dancing and indeed recitations would also be included. Such enthusiasm built up for these visits of the Dancers of Don to London that the expressed sentiment of Moultrie Kelsol, the actor, likening their visits to a green oasis in the arid London desert, was a widely held opinion. The year 1937 also saw the Dancers make history by giving the first-ever television performance of Scottish country dancing from Alexandra Palace, while in 1938 they appeared at the Empire Exhibition, Bellahouston. On their home ground, the Music Hall, Aberdeen, was a regularly used venue, where with the Aberdeen Reel and Strathspey Society, two or three singers, a fiddler and recitations in the Doric, the public could acclaim genuine Scottish entertainment.

The object of the Dancers of Don when demonstrating was to show as many progressions and movements as possible. Much favoured dances were *The New-Rigged Ship, General Stuart's Reel, Montgomery's Rant, Haughs of Cromdale* and, interestingly, the *Reel of Six.*

Most of the Dancers of Don came from families where dancing was in the blood, and they started dancing at an early age. One of them recounts first lessons at the age of five in an outbuilding. 'Walloping' postures were not tolerated by the Dancie, who, having spat on the ground, would command his young pupil to 'dance on that and dinna move aff it!' To the Dancers of Don, incidentally, goes the credit of ladies first appearing as a demonstration team in below-the-calf length white dresses.

The post-war years saw special recognition being given to the group. They attended a Command Performance before the Queen (Princess Elizabeth at the time) and Princess Margaret in the Music

Hall, Aberdeen, and a few years later another Command Performance was given for Princess Margaret in aid of childrens' charities. Another noteworthy appearance was in Glasgow when a foursome gave a private performance at a reception held for Fritz Kreisler, the world famous violinist.

Over a period of twenty years, the Dancers of Don made an unusual impact on the dancing scene. Their record speaks for their artistry. But above all, they seemed to find the route from their dancing to their audiences' hearts. Any group that could finish evenings in spontaneous hymn singing with their audience must have possesssed empathy to a remarkable degree.

TIM WRIGHT AND THE CAVENDISH BAND

With a great working of elbows
The fiddlers ranted.
'Wedding'.   George Mackay Brown (b. 1921)

In the nineteen twenties a young man from Stratford-upon-Avon arrived in Edinburgh.   His occupation was stockbroker's clerk: his hobby was music.   Tim Wright claimed Scottish descent through his father who had instilled into him a love of the old Scottish airs.   As a young man he had sung in the church choir and became an accomplished pianist.   Soon after his arrival in Edinburgh he formed a trio to play in the evenings in a cafe near Tollcross: his career as a musician was now on its way.

Not so far away from the cafe where Tim Wright was playing stood a large riding school and stables.   When jazz and ballroom dancing made their impact in the nineteen twenties a local businessman, seizing an opportunity, made the necessary structural alterations to the building and as Maxim's Dance Hall it was a prominent social gathering place until the thirties when it closed for rather obscure reasons.   In due course it entered new management under the name of The Cavendish.

In the meantime Tim Wright was making his mark.   His original trio had grown to a sizeable band and by the late nineteen thirties the band was well known on radio.   But as he established his position in the country dancing scene he placed increasing emphasis on the inclusion of fiddles in his band as opposed to the growing uptake of accordions in most country dance bands.   It was this emphasis on fiddle music that was to provide him with invitations to play at the country's great balls and to ensure his popularity in the years ahead.   Came the war and nineteen forty saw Tim Wright ensconced

75

as bandleader at the New Cavendish Ballroom, playing the kind of music demanded by war-time audiences. Night after night the Cavendish was packed with service people and the band's popularity grew. At the end of the war Wright took the given opportunity to buy the Cavendish, a move which in due course was to ensure for many years the enjoyment of country dancers in Edinburgh.

Prior to 1950 little Scottish country dancing had taken place at the Cavendish. At that time, though, largely due to the activities of the Scottish Country Dance Society, country dancing became increasingly popular. In his eagerness to see it obtain its full share of prominence in the social scene, Wright set aside every Tueday and Thursday night for country dancing at the Cavendish. Bearing in mind that the Cavendish dancers were enjoying music from the ten-piece band it can hardly be said that profit was his ruling motive. Wright shared with Jean Milligan, founder of the Scottish Country Dance Society, as it then was, the conviction that fiddles were the instruments *par excellence* for country dancing and he recorded on behalf of the Society. The band was now broadcasting every month and playing regularly at the Gathering Balls in Skye, Lochaber, Oban, Inverness and Perth. The band's heavy emphasis on strings ensured its popularity at functions where country dances were mixed with such other dances as waltzes and foxtrots. This period also saw a start being made by Tim Wright and his colleagues to the seeking out and arranging of literally hundreds of long-unplayed tunes by such old masters as the Gows, Marshal and Skinner, thus contributing to their survival.

The dancing public can be as fickle as any other, and by 1959 support for the twice-weekly sessions in the Cavendish was beginning to fade. The sessions were first reduced to one a week in an attempt to keep the country dance connection going, but even this was to prove ineffective and they were eventually phased out. It was indeed a time of change, as in 1959, one year before Tim Wright was to die, Jimmy McIntosh, his deputy and brilliant country dance pianist took over the band and maintained its prominent function list and its reputation in country dance circles over his seven years as leader.   In 1966, Andrew Bathgate, the clarinetist, whose playing had provided body to the fiddle music, took charge and, shunning self-promotion, changed the name of the band to the New Cavendish Band in an attempt to ensure its continuity when he retired.   Andrew Bathgate's association with the band stretched over nearly fifty years and his personal contribution to country dancing in terms of research, scoring and playing has been immense.   It is nice to be able to record that many of the Ball Committees who had enjoyed his playing joined together to present him with a magnificent silver salver in recognition of his contribution when he recently retired.

Today the New Cavendish Band, still with five fiddlers to the fore, maintains its rather unique sound which has made it popular for so many years at its regular round of Hunt, Regimental and Highland Balls.

JOHN DREWRY

No guess could tell what instrument appear'd,
But all the soul of Music's self was heard;
Harmonious concert rung in every part,
While simple melody pour'd moving on the heart.

The Brigs of Ayr. Robert Burns (1759—1796)

Surely, one would think, the composer of dances bearing such proud names as *Bratach Bana, The Quaich,* and *The Peat Fire Flame* must lay claim to origins in some heathery stronghold. But such is not the case. The most brilliant and prolific writer of Scottish country dances alive today, John Drewry, is a Leicestershire man. His childhood was spent in that county whose green fields and trim hedgerows advertise the fact that hunting is the major country pursuit, although some sportsmen will quickly point out the association with one of the most famous rugby clubs in England. Indeed, since the early nineteen hundreds, the 'Tigers' have been the only club in England to have a regular fixture with the Barbarians, the renowned touring side drawing players from all nations.

But music, not hunting or rugby, was the major interest in young John Drewry's life, and in his case the money spent on piano lesons was to be a wise investment. Beethoven, Mozart, Schubert were his early favourites and an affection for and understanding of classical music remains with him; a contributory factor, no doubt, to the precision he is able to build into his compositions.

In due course John Drewry was to become the first student from Leicester Technical College to obtain an external first class honours degree from London University, and 1955 saw him take up an appointment as a chemist at Whitehaven in Cumberland. As one who loves stretching his legs in the country, it was a posting he looked forward to, and soon he was getting to know well the hills of Cumbria. His introduction to the country dance scene was about to happen.   The Rambling Club which John Drewry joined contained a number of Scots.   Frequently at mid-week meetings the members would listen to a talk and then enjoy some country dances.   He found himself in a 'duck takes to water' situation, started to study the dances and in due coure regularly made the long trek to Carlisle to attend an advanced class.

His first composition, he claims, was written more for a joke than anything else, but, encouraged by Hugh Foss, he continued to develop his ideas, and such exciting dances as *Bratach Bana, Peat Fire Flame,* and *Mrs. MacPherson of Inveran* gave a foretaste of what was to come.   His first book of dances was printed in 1962.   Its title *Scottish Country Dances in Traditional Form* was as unpretentious as the publication itself, which was run off on a duplicating machine. One of the dances was given the name *Bon Accord* by the advanced class teacher who hailed from Aberdeen, while *The Bonnie Lass O' Bon Accord* was written for the wedding of a Whitehaven member whose roots also lay in the Granite City.   Somewhat prophetic, one might think, as in due course Drewry was to take up residence in Bon Accord Crescent, Aberdeen.   Inevitably, when the book was re-printed, the opportunity was taken to re-title it *The Bon Accord Book.*

In 1965, just one month before obtaining his Teacher's Certificate from the R.S.C.D.S., John Drewry moved to Aberdeen to take up a University appointment and thus began his long association with the Aberdeen Branch of the Society.

Like Burns, frequently he seeks inspiration for his talents from old Scots tunes, thus helping to keep those beautiful melodies alive.   On other occasions he drafts a dance, leaving it to someone else to provide the music.   Andrew Rankine, for example, composed the music for his *Byron Strathspey* and *Alexandria Reel.*

To date, John Drewry has written more than three hundred and fifty dances.   His compositions seem to be intuitive and inspirational rather than the result of prolonged, painstaking labour.   The Bonnie Lass O' Bon Accord he reckons to have devised in ten minutes, the idea of the unique preamble having been awakened by hearing Jimmy Blair play the tune without an initial chord.   His great reel *Bratach Bana* grew from his love of the tune, although he concedes it may be more difficult to compile a good simple dance than a good difficult one.   One breakthrough, which obviously gives him satisfaction, was the innovation of commencing dances with the third and fourth couples on opposite sides, thus providing dancers with the mental challenge of *A Toast To St. Andrew's* and the enjoyment of *Blooms of Bon Accord.*

If John Drewry had written only *The Bees of Maggieknockater*, his fame would be assured; for *The Bees* is one of the great fun dances.   Maggieknockater is a hamlet in Banffshire, lying about two miles north-east of Craigellachie, and it was the large 'Maggie-knockater Apiary' sign that prompted the idea of the dance.   For the uninitiated, it should be explained that *The Bees* is a dance where, without halting, the dancers change partners at an alarming rate, at the same time carrying out non-stop reels on the sidelines; a cynic once described it as a form of wife-swapping set to music.   Be that as it may, it is a dance that is always eagerly anticipated and there is invariably at least one set that explodes with mirth.   It is nice to recall that one club once used *The Bees* to sting John Drewry into merriment.   In October 1983, while attending a dance in Banff, Alberta, where he had been teaching, a set suddenly took the floor, with the dancers attired in black and yellow striped bee costumes and performed the dance to the strains of Rimsky-Korsakov's 'Flight of the Bumble Bee' while an elderly Queen Bee wielded a tennis racquet to discourage any flagging drone from slacking.   This entertainment the composer was forced to watch through over-sized pink spectacles.

John Drewry, of course, is a man who can integrate a sense of humour into his dances.   Some years ago, a button of some importance departing from a garment of greater importance at 'An Edinburgh Fancy' — the R.S.C.D.S. contribution to the Edinburgh Festival — prompted the dance *The Breeks are Loose and the*

Button's Awa, and *The Haggis Tree* owes its origins to the American lady who accepted its botanical feasibility.

Although John Drewy is an adventurous composer who has given tremendous pleasure with the new progressions and movements he has brought to the dancing scene, his musical taste is, perhaps surprisingly, conservative. His preference is for the older tunes with good phrasing, the more traditional types of band with fiddles rather than accordions, and he does not enthuse overmuch about the use of syncopated chords. Amongst his compositions he ranks *The Alder Burn* highly, but obviously he has more than a soft spot for *The Silver Tassie*. Whether he will devise anything more beautiful than *The Bonnie Lass O' Bon Accord* must remain to be seen. His love of hill walking remains with him, and he has been recognised by more than one dancer in Torridon and in Skye.

The spread of Scottish country dancing thoghout the world delights John Drewry greatly, and he is much in demand by overseas clubs, especially in North America, to attend their functions. The growing enthusiasm amongst the Hong Kong Chinese and Central Europeans for reels, jigs and strathspeys will no doubt encourage further magic from the Drewry pen, and further entries on the computer, where everything is meticulously catalogued.

THE MILITARY CONTRIBUTION

O why the deuce should I repine,
And be an ill foreboder?
I'm twenty three and five feet nine, —
I'll go and be a sodger.
'I'll go and be a Sodger'   Robert Burns (1759—1796)

'I always encourage young officers to frequent balls and assemblies,' wrote General Wolfe, 'it softens their manners and makes them civil.' No doubt that most enlightened soldier had not every regimental dancing occasion in mind when he scribed these words. Dancing can be performed with the maximum of decorum; it can also be the excuse for the rumbustious release of high spirits.

Bernard Fergusson, the great Chindit leader, in his autobiography 'The Trumpet in the Hall' spells out the dancing scene in pre-war days:

'Afterwards there would be dancing: eightsome or sixteen-some reels followed by foursomes, and country dances like the *Duke of Perth* and *Hamilton House*.   Each new officer had to satisfy the Adjutant concerning his proficiency in these, and it was galling for a young Highlander who had danced from his nursery days to the entire satisfaction of his proud family when his performance was judged not up to regimental standard.   There were certain prescribed regimental steps to be mastered too. Undue shouting and skelloching in a reel was pronounced vulgar, and woe betide you if reports came back from the Northern Meeting or the Portree Gathering that you had been seen or heard doing something unbecoming in a reel.'

In stark and hilarious contrast, George MacDonald Fraser's 'The General Danced at Dawn' reveals that hazards may be encountered by soldiers on the dance floor as well as on the battle field:

'Right, Gentlemen, shall we dance?'
This was part of the weekly ritual. We would take off our
tunics, and the pipers would make preparatory whines, and the
Colonel would perch on a table, swinging his game leg which the
Japanese had broken for him on the railway, and would say:
'Now, Gentlemen, as you know, there is Highland dancing as
performed when ladies are present, and there is Highland
dancing. We will have Highland dancing. In Valetta in '21 I
saw a Strip the Willow performed in eighty-nine seconds and an
Eightsome reel in two minutes twenty-two seconds. These are
our targets. All right, pipey.'

This great yarn, which tells of a General guiding his charges
through Eightsome, Sixteensome and Thirty-twosome reels to a
Sixty-foursome and ultimately a Hundred and twenty-eightsome reel,
should be read by all dancers with a sense of humour.

Although there are regimental variations, it can be said that officers
in the Highland regiments are required to be proficient in the
Foursome, Eightsome and Sixteensome reels and to have a good
knowledge of the more popular dances such as *The Duke of Perth,*
Hamilton House, and, of course *The Reel of the 51st Division,* which
first saw the light of day, as *The St. Valery Reel,* in a prisoner of war
camp. Dance practices are held before breakfast for young officers
under the eye of the Pipe Major, and perhaps the adjutant, until it is
deemed the necessary level of proficiency has been reached. Dancing is encouraged amongst other ranks, and inter-regimental competitions take place at organised gatherings.

But of course the Lowland regiments rightly consider country
dancing to be equally their domain. The same range of dances are
learned as in the Highland regiments. Dancing takes place in the
mess after dinner on dining-in nights, and sets will attend the annual
Caledonian Ball in London.

Perhaps the name of the Royal Scots comes to the fore with
dancers. Written many years ago by Pipe Major Denholm, the tune

of the *Royal Scots Polka* is still heard today. Currently, the *Reel of the Royal Scots* is being introduced into many country dance programmes. This dance was first introduced at the officers' ball held to celebrate the three hundred and fiftieth anniversary of the founding of the Regiment; Pipe Major Clark of the 1st Battalion composed the music, while the dance was devised by Roy Goldring. The dance was widely applauded at the Edinburgh Tattoo when it was danced every evening by ladies of the Royal Scottish Country Dance Society partnered by soldiers of the Regiment.

But it is probably in the promoting of Scottish country dancing throughout the world that the military has made its greatest contribution. At overseas stations, regiments may form Reel Clubs which meet weekly to help develop links and foster goodwill with the local population. Demonstrations of dances will be given before guests are offered an opportunity to participate. The quite remarkable popularity of the Reel Clubs is, no doubt one reason why Scottish regiments are such welcome visitors. Many of our Scottish country dances indicate military origins. Some of these, such as the *Dashing White Sergeant, General Stuart's Reel* and *Soldiers Joy* are very old. The *Edinburgh Volunteers* suggests a civilian association with the army. The old military custom of giving numbers to regiments, however, could cause confusion to dancers and was not conducive to extending the life of dances carrying such a title. An obelisk in the Floriana Gardens, Malta, carries the epitaph:

> Here lies the poor old 75th
> But under God's protection
> They'll rise again in kilt and hose
> A glorious resurrection
> For by the transformation powers
> Of Parliamentary Laws
> They go to bed the 75th
> and rise the Ninety-Twas.

While to the army man the 92nd is synonymous with the *Gay Gordons,* it is just as well the strathspey carrying the title of *The Ninety-Second* has the alternative name of *The Marquis of Huntly's Highlanders.*

TARTAN AND DRESS

It is an ancient dress,
a martial dress and a
becoming dress.
Sir Walter Scott (1771—1832)

Inevitably there comes a time when the Scottish country dancer has to dress up. And national costume is an emotive field where experts and pseudo-experts abound — what tartan may be worn; which shoulder for the sash? Just what is traditional dress? A good question when the national dress has shown such variations over the centuries. And who sets the rules? Whoever decided that a black bow tie was *de rigeur* for a formal dinner?

Good taste may be difficult to define but is nevertheless recognisable. But fashions *do* change, evolution applies to dress as to other things. The maintenance of taste can be married to the natural desire of the Scot to dress in a style that expresses individualism in his national dress.

Tartan may be a marketable commodity so far as the tourist trade is concerned, but the regular dancer will want to wear his or her tartan with assurance and an easy conscience. First choice will normally be a clan or family tartan, and if this is not a straight relationship then some research is warranted to establish if a sept link to a clan exists. Where this cannot be identified, there are other choices open for consideration. First, there are a number of district tartans, such as the Lochaber, Crieff and Dundee, for consideration. Some of these district tartans are very old. It must be remembered that while the linkage between a particular pattern and a clan name did not reach any substantial degree of formalisation until after the repeal in 1782 of the 1746 Act of Proscription, which forbade the wearing of Highland dress, there is considerable evidence that certain patterns or setts were associated with a given locality for many centuries previously. Admittedly, the bulk of the people in the locality would be expected to have a clan relationship, nevertheless it was the badge of the clan, such a sprig of heath or fir that orginally identified membership of a clan, and not the tartan. Long term residence in one of these districts, therefore, overcomes the obstacle for those not possessing a tartan-bearing name.

Next, in choice of a tartan, one can proclaim one's politics — the Jacobite tartan for those families that were 'out' in the '45 and the Black Watch for the government orientated. The beautiful Caledonian tartan is another possibility and, as a search through sample books will show, there are a number of tartans of unrecorded origins and without names which can be confidently worn. Strictly, a mother's tartan should not be worn unless her name is taken, as this would suggest allegiance to another clan chief. The male dancer has another two points to bear in mind when buying a kilt: the hunting tartans are best avoided for social wear (in case such action be misconstrued!) and care should be taken with the dress tartans. In 'Highland Evening Fling', by Lt. Col. Iain Taylor, who has for many years been regarded as highly authoritative on dress, opines that dress patterns were designed originally for ladies who preferred lighter-coloured patterns. Queen Victoria, who is reputed to have substituted white for red in the Royal Stewart, was, according to Iain Taylor, displaying knowledge of tartan, for her new design was in the tradition of the old arisaid setts for head shawls and dresses. Anyway, the position today is quite confusing and gentlemen are safer to avoid tartans with white as a forcible colour.

The original form of trews, cut on the bias and leg-hugging, are just as authentic a form of highland wear as the kilt, but have no appeal today as a form of dress. The wearing of trews, along with the kilt, was forbidden by the Act of Proscription, and, after its repeal, trews were not to recover their original popularity. Frequently used when horseriding, early nineteenth century paintings such as 'Sporting

Meeting' show their replacement, when mounted, by very narrow tartan trousers. The painting of 'The Shamit Reel', which illustrated the dancing of a Foursome reel at a wedding in the Elgin district in 1836, shows narrow tartan trousers worn with a diced balmoral by one of the guests. Neil Gow, of course, was well known for his tartan breeches and hose. When George IV visited Edinburgh in 1822, jacket and trouser suits in tartan were in evidence, and indeed one such outfit, with small shoulder plaid, may be seen in the fascinating Museum of Scottish Tartans in Comrie, Perthshire. The tartan trousers, miscalled trews, worn by Scottish regiments, are a purely army introduction. But one wonders if, with now around two hundred years of history behind them, the use of such trousers as a dress for social occasions has not been neglected. Certainly their wear with a mess jacket would be more enhancing than the standard-ised penguin dinner attire that removes individuality.

Ladies, of course, do not wear a kilt, if only on the grounds that its cut does not flatter the female form. The sash is the most interesting piece of female tartan apparel. It should be worn over the right shoulder and fastened to the left hip, unless the wearer happens to be the wife of a clan chief or of the colonel of a Highland regiment, when it is worn on the left shoulder. Ladies, when married, adopt their husband's tartan. If he does not have the right to a tartan, then she wears her own tartan, when the sash, still worn over the right shoulder, should be knotted at the ends and hung on the left hip.

Sir Thomas Innes of Learney, the late Lord Lyon King of Arms, has some simple instructions on dress for ladies:

> For evening wear, a skirt of tartan silk or other light material is worn with any suitable corsage, usually decorated with Celtic embroidery and the graceful arisaid of silk hangs down the back and is gathered on the breast by a Celtic or Heraldic Brooch. Sometimes the smaller tonnag or shoulder shawl of tartan silk or light woven material is similarly worn. With ordinary evening dress a sash is worn across the right shoulder, fastened by a

badge-brooch. Such sashes look best when fairly voluminous. The 'Aboyne'dress is one of the most beautiful forms of Highland Formal Dress.

Certainly no-one will argue with that last sentence. The laced corsage and wide-sleeved blouse of the 'Aboyne' exudes an enchantment that surpasses all other forms of ladies' wear. There is a well-known painting of Flora MacDonald wearing a tartan dress of chiffon or similar material. One wonders if the ladies of today are not a little too conservative in dress when ballroom bound.

Many books have been written on the paraphernalia connected with evening wear to be worn at large social gatherings. Plaids and dirks have left the scene, and, happily, few goat hair sporrans are still in existence. But at present it has to be recognised that most country dancing takes place in specialist clubs, branches of the Royal Scottish Country Dance Society and evening classes. The thousands who dance every week will attend few balls. Dress at completely informal functions presents no difficulties. Belts are not worn with kilts and simple skirts and blouses or dresses are appropriate for ladies. It is the slightly up-market function that raises the issues. A white shirt and a tie with a kilt presents a highly acceptable picture. It is a personal view, but how much more colourful the scene would be if ladies would adopt a version of the 'Aboyne' for these occasions.

Turning to less important items, it has to be said that many sporrans today are abominations, quite incapable of carrying the minimum of essentials. Credit must be given to the few enterprising craftsmen who are now producing sporrans, based on old styles, with an appropriate capacity.

One deprecates, too, the habit of some male dancers of pulling their hose right up to the knees. The lack of gap between kilt and hose is not a pretty sight and is not in the Highland tradition. It is better if dancers remember the old army adage that the top of the hosetop should be worn 'a handsbreadth below the kneecap.' The current vogue for white stockings, promoted perhaps by dress hire companies, requires to be kept under control.   While white stockings are not wrong apparel, any self colour is acceptable, and many colours, such as claret or fawn or green, provide a more tasteful contrast to the kilt and doublet than white.   Matching dice-patterned stocking are, of course, the ideal wear but their price today verges on the prohibitive. Care should be taken to avoid any hose knitted so as to create the impression of thickening the leg to a distorted degree.

One notices the total commitment nowadays to dancing slippers for country dancing in specialist clubs.   It is not so many years ago that such pumps were considered appropriate only for Highland dancers appearing in competitions.   Studies of old time dancers show that their regular footwear was either patent leather shoes or normal outdoor shoes, while ladies would wear shoes with a small heel.   No doubt the move to pumps is merely another example of evolution in dress.   And if pumps are to be worn by gentlemen, the laces should be tied 'gillie' fashion, with their bow-knot at the side of the leg and not wrapped round the foot like a sprinter's spikes.   Untidy laces discredit the garb.   Laces around the ankle are not becoming to the female leg and draw-strings in the shoes are much to be preferred. Country dancing, even with the restricted range of sixteen dances so often encountered today, is still substantial exercise and anything that lightens the load will find its followers.

One final point about the wearing of the kilt.   It is the most impressive of all national costumes, but to be seen at its best, the wearer must sport it in comfort and with confidence.   Those then, who were not brought up to wear the kilt, should make use of it on other than dancing occasions and thereby develop the necessary 'carry' which declares its superiority over all other kinds of dress.

COUNTRY DANCING
IN PROSE AND VERSE

In a land so devoted to dancing it is not surprising to find such a large amount of reference to it in our literature. Many of the quotations my research has turned up are not only entertaining but also highly interesting because of the insight they give us into the social attitudes prevalent at the time of their writing.

In this section I have set out, in chronological order, a collection of gems which, in their own way, tell a story of Scotland, as much as of dancing, over the centuries.

While it is difficult, if not impossible, to identify the first chronicler of dancing, we can at least thank Dunbar, who was born somewhwere around 1460, for letting us know in *'The Twa Mariit Wemen'* that dancing through the night is not a recent phenomenon:

> *Thus draif they out that dear night with dances full noble,*
> *Till that the day did up daw, and dew donkit the flouris.*

The rollicking *Peblis to the Play* which tells the story of Peebles at fair-time, is an early poem which cannot be ascribed with assurance. If it is based on fact, the conclusion must be drawn that there were few inhibitions, if any, displayed when it came to responding to music!:

> *They gadderit out of the toun,*
> *And nearer him they dreuch;*
> *And bade gife the danceris room;*
> *Will Swane makis wonder teuch.*
> *Then all the wenches Te he! they play it;*
> *Bot Lord, as Will Young leuch!*
> *'Gude gossip, come hyne yon gatis;*
> *For we have dansit aneuch,*
> > *at anis,*
> *At Peblis to the Play'.*

By the time *The Complaynt of Scotland,* that amazing record of Scottish life by Sir David Lyndsay, was written in 1549, it is obvious that dancing was a well-entrenched pastime. Some thirty dances are recorded in *The Complaynt,* and some of their names would not be out of place today: *Tom of Linn, Soutra, Hunt's Up, The Loch of Slene, The Bee, Inverness.*

On the other hand, some names *would* be out of place today: *The Lamb's Wind, Come kittle me naked wantonly, Shake leg foot before gossep.*

But times were changing. Within a few years the Reformation was having its effect on such simple pleasures as dancing and men like Sir Richard Maitland were to look back on the good old days with obvious nostaligia:

> *Quhair is the blythness that hes bein*
> *Bayth in brugh and landwart sein.*
> *Amang lordis and ladies schien,*
> *Dansing, singing, game and play?*
> *Bot weill I wot nocht quhat they mein;*
> *All merriness is worne away.*

In 1561, Mary, Queen of Scots, arrived in Scotland. Life in the French court had developed within her a love of dancing. Alas, she was not to have an ally in John Knox:

> Of dancing, Madam, I said that, albeit in the scriptures I found no praise of it, and in profane writers that it is termed the gesture rather of those that are mad and in frenzy than of sober men; yet I do not utterly condemn it, providing that two vices be avoided: (Firstly) that the principal vocation of those that use that exercise must not be neglected for the pleasure of dancing; (secondly) that they dance not, as did the Philistines their fathers, for the pleasure that they take in the displeasure of God's people. If they do either, they shall receive the reward of dancers, and that will be to drink in Hell, unless they speedily repent, and so shall God turn their mirth into sudden sorrow.

The Queen's comment *'Ye are over-sair for me'*, can be understood! But Knox had given the Church a lead. Pleasures were the work of the devil; in modern parlance, it was time to put the clerical boot in. Tom Johnston in his *History of the Working Classes in Scotland* reminds us:

> Absence from Kirk was a sin; drinking during times of sermon, dancing, kissing a maid on the causeway, watering kail and playing bogill about the stooks on the Sabbath, were the causes of God's wrath.

So the sixteen-hundreds wore on with scant reference in their early years to dancing in Scottish literature, although mention of witches and music in association are to be found. Yet something was stirring; the movement of the court to London may have removed the focal and leading cultural point from Scotland, but it did encourage, if not force, the ordinary people to develop their own cultural instincts and this, inevitably, meant expresion in music and dance. Slowly the playing of the fiddle and cello became more common, and in 1679 attitudes had so changed that in Edinburgh, a dancing master was allowed to practice. In 1700 the first printed collection of Scottish music was published, in London.

Having been through a dancing Dark Age, the eighteenth century saw the Scots take to their own national form of dancing as few, if any, other countries have ever done. We are obliged to Chambers in his *Traditions of Edinburgh* for so succintly covering the metamorphosis:

> Everything that could be called public or promiscuous amusement was held in abhorrence by the Presbyterians, and only struggled through a desultory and degraded existence by the favour of the Jacobites, who have always been a less strait-laced part of the community. Thus, there was nothing like a conventional system of dancing in Edinburgh till the year 1710, when at length a private association was commenced under the name of 'The Assembly.'

But the movement back to dancing was not to be sudden, and the

Assemblies were certainly not popular to begin with. Epithets such as 'Herodias' and 'Jezebel' were frequently hurled at the dancers. But Allan Ramsay, ever ready to support anything that afforded amusement, lifted his pen in defence:

Sic as against the Assembly speak,
The rudest sauls betray
When matrons noble, wise and meek,
Conduct the healthfu' play
Where they appear nae vice daur keek,
But to what's guid gies way,
Like night, sune as the morning creek
Has ushered in the day.

Alas, it was to take more than Ramsay's enthusiasm to bring jollity to the dancing. Goldsmith in his visit to an Assembly in 1753, depicts a dullness and separation of the sexes few dancers would believe;

Let me say something of their balls, which are very frequent here. When a stranger enters the dancing-hall, he sees one end of the room taken up with the ladies, who sit dismally in a group by themselves; on the other end stand their pensive partners that are to be; but no more intercourse between the sexes than between two countries at war. The ladies, indeed, may ogle, and the gentlemen sigh, but an embargo is laid upon any closer commerce.

But if the population of Edinburgh had not yet come to terms with dancing, there was no doubt about the liveliness of dances in the country. Alexander Ross, the Angus schoolmaster whose gravestone still stands sentinel over the cold waters of Loch Lee, could happily describe a typical scene:

Fan they hae done wi' eating o't,
Fan they hae done wi' eating o't,
For dancing they gae to the green,
And aiblins to the beatin' o't;

He dances best that dances fast,
And loups at ilka reesing o't,
And claps his hands frae 'hough' to 'hough',
And furls about the feezings o't.

Further south, the Traquair diaries were to indicate the commitment of the Border aristocracy to country dancing:

16th December, 1782. Lord and Lady Traquair and Louisa went to Ball at Town House, Peebles. Louisa opened the Ball with a hornpipe, danced the first country dance with Gilbert Kennedy and second with James Honeyman. Lady Traquair danced two country dances with Mr. Robert. Lord Traquair danced two dances with Miss Hamilton.

But of course the Assemblies were to find themselves. The minuets gave way to reels and strathspeys, and, as Mrs. Cockburn was happily to record, the gentlemen of the day were to take more than a passing interest in their partners:

Nancy's to the Assembly gone
To hear the fops a-chattering;
And Willie he has followed her,
To win her love by flattering.

Wad ye hae bonnie Nancy?
Na, I'll hae ane was learned to fence,
An' that can please my fancy,
Ane that can flatter, bow and dance,
an' mak' love to the ladies;
That kens how folk behave in France,
An's bauld among the caddies.

No study of the literature of country dancing of the period towards the end of the eighteenth century can ignore the many mentions made of dancing by Burns in his poems and songs: *Tam O'Shanter, Reel o' Stumpie, Tam Glen, The Ploughman, The De'ils Awa* and of course the glorious Jolly Beggars are just a few that contain references. But

96

Lockhart, in his classic biography of the Bard, reminds us that Burnes, Senior, Robert's father, was, at least initially, not over keen to see his son develop such social talents:

He had indeed that dislike of dancing-schools which Robert mentions; but so far overcame it during Robert's first month of attendance, that he permitted the rest of the family that were fit for it, to accompany him during the second month. Robert excelled in dancing, and was for some time distractedly fond of it.

Such indeed was Burns's enthusiasm for dancing that, according to Lockhart, he was, at least on one occasion, persuasive enough to entice the members of the Bachelors' Club to trip 'the light fantastic':

'On one solitary occasion,' says he (Burns), 'we resolved to meet at Tarbolton in July, on the race-night, and have a dance in honour of our society. Accordingly, we did meet, each one with a partner, and spent the night in such innocence and merriment, such cheerfulness and good humour, that every brother will long remember it with delight.'

Yet it was not to be Burns, but Carolina, Baroness Nairne, who was to present the world with the most descriptive poem ever written on country dancing. Such is its quality, *'County Meeting'* is worth setting out in full:

Ye're welcome, leddies, ane and a'
Ye're welcome to our County Ha';
Sae weel ye look when buskit braw
To grace our County Meeting!
An', Gentlemen, ye're welcome too,
In waistcoats white and tartan too,
Gae seek a partner, mak' yer bow,
Syne dance our County Meeting.

Ah, weel dune now, there's auld Sir John
Who aye maun lead the dancin' on,

97

An' Leddy Bet, wi' her turban prim.
An' wee bit velvet 'neath her chin;
See how theuy nimbly, nimbly go!
While youngsters follow in a row,
Wi' mony a belle an' mony a beau,
To dance our County Meeting.

There's the Major, and his sister too,
He in the bottle-green, she in the blue;
(Some years sin' syne that gown was new
At our County Meeting.)
They are a worthy, canty pair,
An' unco proud o' their nephew Blair,
O' sense or siller he's nae great share,
Tho' he's the King o' the Meeting.

An' there's our Member, and provost Whig,
Our doctor in his yellow wig,
Wi' his fat wife, wha takes a jig
Aye at our County Meeting.
MissBetty, too, I see her there,
Wi' her sonsy face and bricht red hair,
Dancin' till she can dance nae mair
At our County Meeting.

There's beauty Belle wha a' surpasses,
An' heaps o' bonnie country lasses,
Wi' the heiress o' the Gowdenlea —
Folk say she's unco dorty.
Lord Bawbee aye he's lookin' there,
An' sae is the Major and Major's heir,
Wi' the Laird, the Shirra, an' mony mair,
I could reckon them to forty.

See Major O'Neill has got her hand,
An' in the dance they've ta'en their stand
('Impudence comes frae Paddy's land!'
Say the lads o' our County Meeting);
But ne'er ye fash, gang thro' the reel,
The country-dance, ye dance sae weel
An' ne'er let waltz or dull quadrille
Spoil our County Meeting.

Afore we end, strike up the spring
O' Thulican and Hieland fling,
The Haymakers and Bumpkin fine,
At our County Meeting.
Gow draws his bow, folk haste away,
While some are glad and some are wae,
A' blithe to meet some ither day
At our County Meeting.

But now the established country dances had to prove their
mettle.   The years around the end of the eighteenth and the early part
of the nineteenth centuries saw the introduction into this country from
the continent of dances such as the Waltz, the Polka, Lancers and
Quadrilles.   Tempers flared as dancers debated whether or not such
foreign invasion should be welcomed.   The heart of John Skinner
beat fast under the clerical garb as it rejected the invaders:

There needs na' be sae great a phrase,
Wi' dringing dull Italian lays,
I wadna gie our ain Strathspeys,
For half a hundred score o' 'em.
They're dowff and dowie at the best,
Dowff and dowie, dowff and dowie,
They're dowff and dowie at the best,
Wi' a' their variorum.

They're dowff and dowie at the best,
Their allegros and all the rest,
They canna please a Scottish taste,
Compar'd wi' Tullochgorum.

Alex. MacRae, curator of the Clan Donnachaidh Museum at Struan recounts the lines handed down in his family:
Droch bhas air jigs quadrille's waltz
(Bad death on jigs, quadrilles and the waltz)
A thug a ghraisg a nall a France
(Brought by the riff-raff over from France)
God Bless the Queen she likes to dance
Ruidhle Mor Strathspe,
(The big reel from Strathspey).

But, as has been pointed out, sides were taken.   Elizabeth Grant of Rothiemurchus, whose *Memoirs of a Highland Lady* represent one of the finest social studies of Scotland in the nineteenth century, has much to say in favour of at least one continental introduction:
1816—1817.   There were very few large balls given this winter.   A much more pleasant style of smaller parties had come into fashion with the new style of dancing.   It was the first season of quadrilles, against the introduction of which there had been great stand made by old-fashioned respectables.   Many resisted the new French figures altogether, and it was a pity to give up the merry country dance, in which the warfare between the two opinions resulted; but we young people were all bit by the quadrille mania, and I was one of the set that brought them first into notice.   We practised privately; and having kept our secret well, we burst upon the world at a select reunion at the White Melvilles', the spectators standing on the chairs and sofas to admire us.   People *danced* in those days; we did not merely stand and talk, look about bewildered for our vis-a-vis, return to

our partners either too soon or too late, without any regard to the completion of the figure, the conclusion of the measure, or the step belonging to it; we attended to our business, moved in cadence, easily and quietly, embarrassing no one and appearing to advantage ourselves.

In the end, the continental dances were to find a home in Scotland. The Polka and the ladies' chain, which is featured in the Quadrilles, becoming standard country dance movements.

Undoubtedly one of the greatest and most readily recognisable reel tunes is *Kate Dalrymple*. But who was Kate? Where did she come from? It was towards the middle of last century that William Watt launched her on the world:

> *In a wee cot-house far across the muir,*
> *Where the peesweeps, plovers and whaups cry dreary,*
> *There lived an auld maid for mony lang years*
> *Wham ne'er a wooer did e'er ca' his dearie.*
> *A lanely lass was Kate Dalrymple,*
> *A thrifty quean was Kate Dalrymple;*
> *Nae music, exceptin' the clear burnie's wimple*
> *Was heard round the dwellin' o' Kate Dalrymple.*

The second half of the nineteenth century saw many references to country dancing at balls and the major meetings. Pride of place, of course, must go to Queen Victoria, who, in *Leaves from the Journal of Our Life in the Highlands*, published in 1868, and its later companion volume *More Leaves from the Journal of Our Life in the Highlands*, showed, by her consistent and lengthy entries her great enthusiasm for country dancing:

September 10, 1852. We dined at a quarter-past six o'clock in morning gowns (not ordinary ones, but such as are worn at a 'breakfast'), and at seven started for Corriemulzie, for a torch-light ball in the open air. I wore a white bonnet, a grey water silk, and, (according to Highland fashion) my plaid scarf over my shoulder: and Albert his Highland dress which he wears

101

every evening. We drove in the postchaise; the two ladies, Lord Derby and Colonel Gordon following in the other carriage.

It was a mild though threatening evening, but fortunately it kept fine. We arrived there at half-past eight, by which time, of course, it was quite dark. Mr and Lady Agnes Duff received us at the door, and then took us at once through the house to the open space where the ball was, which was hid from our view till the curtains were drawn asunder. It was really a beautiful and most unusual sight. All the company were assembled there. A space about one hundred feet in length and sixty feet in width was boarded, and entirely surrounded by Highlanders bearing torches, which were placed in sockets, and constantly replenished. There were seven pipers playing together, Mackay leading — and they received us with the usual salute and three cheers, 'Nis! Nis! Nis!' (pronounced 'Neesh! Neesh! Neesh!, the Highland Hip! Hip! Hip!) and again cheers; after which came a most animated reel. There were above sixty people exclusive of the Highlanders, of whom there were also sixty; all the Highland gentlemen, and any who were at all Scotch, were in kilts, the ladies in evening dresses. The company and the Highlanders danced pretty nearly alternately. There were two or three sword dances. We were upon a *Haut pas*, over which there was a canopy. The whole thing was admirably done, and very well worth seeing. Albert was delighted with it. I must not omit to mention a reel danced by eight Highlanders holding torches in their hands. We left at half-past nine o'clock, and were home by a little past eleven. A long way certainly (fourteen miles I believe.).

September 24th. 1875. At a quarter-past ten we drove across to the temporary pavilion, where the ball to the tenants (of the Duke of Argyll) was to take place. Louise, Beatrice and Jane Churchill went with me in the Duke's coach. The Duke,

Lorne and Colin received us, and the Duchess and all the girls and the other ladies were inside at the upper end on a raised platform, where we all sat.   It is a very long and handsome room, I believe a hundred and thirty feet long, and was built at the time of Louise's marriage.   It was handsomely decorated with flags, and there were present between seven and eight hundred people - tenants with their wives and families, and many people from the town, but it was not like the Highland balls I have been accustomed to, as there were many other dances besides reels.   The band could not play reels (which were played by the piper) and yet came from *Glasgow!*   The ball began, however, with a reel; then came a country dance, then another reel.   Louise danced a reel with Brown, and Beatrice with one of the Duke's foresters; but the band could only play a country dance tune for it.   Another reel with pipes, in which Jane Churchill danced with Brown, and Francie Clark with Annie (Mrs. MacDonald, my wardrobe maid)), Louise and Beatrice dancing in another reel with one of the other people and Mr. John Campbell.   Then came a 'schottische' which seemed to be much liked there, and more reels, and lastly a *'tempete'*, in which Louise and Beatrice danced.....After the *'tempete'* we came away at nearly half-past twelve.

At the other end of the social spectrum we can listen to Scott Skinner as he describes the barns where, as a young lad, he played for dancing:

The barns in which the dancing took place had earthen floors and were not always quite level.   Planks laid on sacks of corn turned on their sides formed the sitting accommodation. Tallow dips mounted on wooden brackets on the walls supplied the lighting, candles not being introduced until about ten years later.....

After several hours dancing, refreshments were served. These consisted of ginger wine for the ladies and whisky 'toddy'

for the men.   Bread and cheese were carried round and served
out from a riddle, which was made presentable by a wide white
cloth......

About four o'clock in the morning the ball broke up.....

I often wonder how I, a boy of eight or nine years, survived the
physical strain and the loss of sleep which my duties with the
band occasioned.   It was nothing unusual for Peter and me to
trudge eight or ten weary miles on a slushy wet night in order to
fulfil a barn engagement.

So we reach the present century where references to contry dancing
are perhaps less prolific.   In *Cloud Howe* Lewis Grassic Gibbon
poses a question that, no doubt, many ladies have asked of themselves:
The next dance she had was with Ogilvie the joiner,.....he swung
her round and round, his own eyes half-closed near all that
time.   If he thought your face such a scunner to look at, why did
he ask you up for a dance?

While Scots will always be grateful to Neil Munro for giving them
Para Handy, it is doubtful if that loveable character's song, *The
Dancing Master* will do much to improve their dancing:
> *Set to Jeanie Mertin,*
> *Up the back and doon the muddle,*
> *Ye're wrong, Jeck, I'm certain.*

In *The Pawky Duke*, David Rorie takes us back in time with lines
that are worth remembering:
> *Then aye afore he socht his bed*
> *He danced the Gillie Callum*
> *An' wi's Kilmarnock owre his neb*
> *What evil could befall him!*

But in a book containing so many personal reminiscences there is a
magnetic pull to conclude with the poem that brings alive joyful
memories of early dancing days:

THE BARN DANCE
W.D. Cocker.

Hey! for the music o' Baldy Bain's fiddle!
Redd up the barn, an' we'll gie ye a reel.
In till it, noo! wi' a diddle-dum-diddle,
Dod! that's the tune to pit springs in your heel.

Skirlin' o' lassocks, an' 'Hoochs' frae ilk fellow,
Cheers, when the gudeman himsel' taks the flair,
Leads Petronella wi' hellicate Bella,
Brawest o' dochters, though gey deil-may-care.

Hey! for the music o' Baldy Bain's fiddle!
Lads frae the bothies, an' herds frae the hill
Cleek wi' young lassies, sae jimp roon the middle.
Gosh! but some auld anes are soople anes still.
Lang Geordie Craddock, the grieve o' Kilmadock,
Widowed sae aft he's fain to forget,
Wha would jalouse he could loup like a puddock?
Faith! but there's spunk in the auld deevil yet!

Hey! for the music o' Baldy Bain's fiddle!
Syne we'll hae supper, for time's wearin' on;
Drinks for the drouthy, an' scones frae the griddle —
Bella's the lass that can bake a guid scone.
Baldy's in fettle, an' sweers he maun ettle
Ae hinmaist hoolachan juist for the last.
Cast yer coats, callans, an' yoke tae't wi' mettle;
Dancin' and daffin' days sune will be past.

THE TWELVE DANCES
EVERY SCOT SHOULD KNOW

There are many hundreds of Scottish country dances and although some individuals with data-bank minds appear capable of reeling off their steps and progressions without difficulty, most lesser mortals require some reference material.   Nevertheless, there are around a dozen Scottish dances that all should know and be able to dance competently.   There is something lacking about a wedding without an Eightsome; and what better way to get a party going than to dance a Dashing White Sergeant?

While my top twelve are very much a personal selection, I doubt if there will be overmuch disagreement with my choice.   For the sake of brevity, dancing terms have been used, and I have provided a glossary for the use of those not acquainted with all the terminology, or perhaps suffering from a little mental rustiness.   My object in so doing is to prime the pump.   Readers wishing to make themselves more aware of the finer points of our country dances should refer to publications of the Royal Scottish Country Dance Society and the Society's official manual *'Won't You Join The Dance?'* by the late Dr. Jean Milligan.   The Society has its headquarters in Coates Cresent, Edinburgh.

But please learn the dances I have given you, if they are not already known to you, and use them at your social occasions: they will never, ever, let you down.   And having learned them, learn another twelve: a whole world of superb entertainment awaits you.

THE EIGHTSOME REEL
Type: Reel — 464 bars.
Formation: Square Set.
The greatest, longest, rowdiest, most diabolically executed of all the

Scottish country dances. Devised by the Duke of Atholl and some friends in the latter part of the last century, it is probably the dance for which Scots have the most affection.

Bars

1—8   All circle eight hands round and back.

9—12   Cartwheel clockwise, ladies joining right hands in the centre.

13—16   Cartwheel anti-clockwise, men joining left hands in the centre.

17—20   Set twice to partners.

21—24   Swing partners or turn partners both hands.

25—40   Grand chain (men moving anti-clockwise and ladies clockwise). The dancing of this chain too quickly is a main reason for chaos ensuing in an Eightsome Reel.

41—88   First lady goes into the centre and dances on her own while the remainder dance seven hands round and back.
First lady sets to her partner and turns him.
First lady sets to opposite man and turns him.
First lady and the two men she has set to and turned dance a reel of three across the dance.
First lady remains in the centre and dances on her own while remainder dance seven hands round and back.
First lady sets to the man on her partner's right and turns him.
First lady sets to the man opposite and turns him.
First lady and the two men she has just set to and turned dance a reel of three across the dance.
First lady returns to original place.

89—232   The movements in bars 41—88 are now repeated in turn by second, third and fourth ladies.

233—424 The movements in bars 41—232 are then repeated in turn by first, second, third and fourth men dancing with the appropriate ladies.

425—464 Repeat bars 1—40.

BROUN'S REEL or THE DUKE OF PERTH

Type: Reel — 32 bars.
Formation: Longwise Set.
Bars
1—4   First couple turn each other with their right hands and cast off on their own sides.
5—8   First couple turn each other with their left hands finishing facing their first corners.
9—10   First couple turn first corners with right hands.
11—12 First couple turn each other with left hands finishing facing second corners.
13—14 First couple turn second corners with right hands.
15—16 First couple turn each other with left hands finishing facing first corners.
17—20 First couple set to and turn first corners with both hands.
21—24 First couple set to and turn second corners with both hands.
25—30 Reels of three on the sides of the dance, first lady dancing the reel on the mens' side and first man dancing the reel on the ladies' side.
31—32 First couple return to own side of the dance one place down.

HAMILTON HOUSE

Type: Jig — 32 bars.
Formation: Longwise Set.
This dance should be performed throughout with *pas de basque.*

Bars
1—4   First lady sets to second man, turns third man with both hands and takes up position between the two men.
5—8   First man sets to second lady, turns third lady with both hands and takes up position between the third couple (while first

woman moves to a position between second couple).

9—12 Join hands in threes and set twice.

13—16 First couple, joining both hands, complete a three-quarter turn finishing on their opposite sidelines between second and third couples.

17—20 Join hands in threes and set twice.

21—24 First couple, joining both hands, turn each other to seond place on own sides of the dance.

25—32 First three couples dance six hands round and back.

MONYMUSK

Type: **Strathspey — 32 bars.**
Formation: **Longwise set.**

Bars

1—4 First couple turn right hands and cast off one place.

5—8 First couple complete a one and a quarter turn with left hands, finishing with the man between the third couple facing up the dance and the lady between the second couple facing down the dance.

9—10 First lady joins hands with the second couple and first man with the third couple and, facing each other up and down the dance, they all set.

11—12 All drop hands and second and third couples set again while first couple dance out to opposite sidelines — first man finishing between second and third ladies and first lady finishing between second and third man.

13—16 First lady and second and third men and first man and second and third ladies join hands on the sidelines and set twice.

17—24 All three couples circle six hands round and back.

25—30 Six bar reels of three on the sides of the dance, first lady dancing the reel on the men's side and beginning the reel by passing third man right shoulder and first man dancing the reel on the ladies' side and beginning by passing second lady right shoulder.

31—32 First couple cross over to second place on their own sides.

DASHING WHITE SERGEANT

Type: Reel — 32 bars
Formation: Round the room dance in three, with half the groups going clockwise and half anti-clockwise, forming dancing sets of six.

Bars
1—8   All dance six hands round and back.
9—12   Man or lady in centre of the three sets to and turns the person on his or her right.
13—16   Man or lady in centre of the three sets to and turns the person on his or her left.
17—24   Each group on its own dances a reel of three.
25—28   Centre person joins hands with his or her partners and all advance to meet opposite group and retire.
29—32   All advance once again and dance through opposite group ready to repeat the dance with the next group of three.

PETRONELLA

Type: Reel— 32 bars.
Formation: Longwise Set.
Bars
1—4   First couple petronella turn to the right to face each other up and down the dance and set.
5—8   First couple petronella turn to the right to face each other across the dance on opposite sides and set.
9—12   Repeat bars 1—4.

13—16   First couple petronella turn to the right back to places on
their own sides of the dance and set.

17—24   First couple lead down the middle of the dance and up again
to original positions.

25—32   First and second couple poussette, the first couple finishing
in second position on their own sides of the dance.

SCOTTISH REFORM

Type: Jig — 32 bars.

Formation: Longwise Set.

Bars

1—4   First couple half turn each other with right hands and join
hands with second couple to form a line across the dance;
men facing down and ladies facing up and all four set.

5—8   First couple drop their right hands and turn the person on
their left into the centre.   All four join hands and set.

9—12   Second couple, who are in the centre, drop their right
hands.   First couple turn the person on their left to return
again to the centre of the dance between second couple.
All four join hands and set.

13—16   First couple, dropping left hands, turn each other with right
hands to return to their original positions.

16—24   First couple lead down the middle of the dance and up
again.

25—32   First and second couple poussette, first couple finishing in
second place on their own sides of the dance.

CIRCASSIAN CIRCLE

Type: Reel — 32 bars.

Formation: Couples face each other for a round the room dance;
ladies on partner's right.

Bars
1—8   All dance rights and lefts.
9—12   All set twice to partners.
13—16   All swing partners (or turn both hands if you want to be posh!).
17—24   Ladies' chain.
25—32   Poussette round opposite couple to meet next advancing pair.

THE GLASGOW HIGHLANDERS

Type: Strathspey — 32 bars.
Formation: Longwise Set.
This dance starts with two chords instead of the customary one. On the second chord, the first lady crosses over diagonally to stand on her partner's right. The second man crosses straight over to occupy his partner's position as she steps up to occupy the place vacated by the first lady.

Bars
1—8   Rights and Lefts.
9—12   Second man finishes the Rights and Lefts by dancing in between first and second ladies and joins hands with them, all facing down the dance. First man takes up position immediately behind second man. All dance down the middle of the set.
13—16   Lead up the dance, first man now between first and second ladies and second man following. Finish across the dance — ladies on sidelines, men on inside facing their partners.
17—24   Set to partners.
25—32   Reel of four across the dance, first couple finishing on the men's side of the dance while second couple return to own sides in first place. On bar 31, the third man crosses over to his partner's place as she moves up into second place.

LA TEMPETE

Type: Reel — 48 bars.

Formation: Four couple progressive. First and second couples take up positions across the dance opposite third and fourth couples, ladies on partners' right.

Bars

1—8 First and fourth couples advance diagonally and dance four hands across with right hands and back with left hands.

9—16 Second and third couples repeat bars 1—8.

17—24 All set twice to partners and turn partners both hands.

25—28 Retaining hands, couples slip step (scoosh!) up or down the dance, men passing back to back.

29—32 Slip step return to place, ladies passing back to back.

33—40 First and third couples and second and fourth couples dance four hands round to the left and return to places giving left hands across.

41—44 All advance, retire and clap three times.

45—48 First and second couples dance under arch made by third and fourth couples, ready to repeat the dance with advancing couples.

LA RUSSE

Type: Reel — 64 bars.

Formation: Square Set.

Bars

1—8 All four couples set to partners and cross right hands to finish facing corners. All set to and turn corners both hands.

9—16 All set to partners twice and turn partners both hands one and a half times.

17—24 First couple promenade round inside of set.

25—32 First couple poussette round inside of set.

33—40 First and third couples change places, first couple dancing

113

between third couple, and return to places, third couple dancing between first couple.

41—48 Repeat bars 33—40.

49—56 Eight hands round to the left.

57—64 All four couples cartwheel in a clockwise direction, ladies joining right hands in the centre.

Second, third and fourth couples repeat the dance.

FOURSOME REEL

Type: Medley — Normally 128 bars, but can be varied provided the component Strathspey and Reel bars are equal.

Formation: Two couple dance. The dance starts with couples facing each other, the lady standing on her partner's right.

Strathspey Time

Bars

1—8 Reel of four across the dance, ladies start the reel by passing left shoulders and men do not commence the dance until Bar 3. At the end of the reel, the ladies should finish in their own places and the men back to back in the centre facing the opposite ladies.

9—16 All set.

17—24 Reel of four across the dance. At the end of the reel, the ladies should finish in their own places and the men back to back in the centre facing their own partners.

25—32 All set.

33—64 Repeat bars 1—32

Reel Time

65—72 Ladies dance two pas-de-basque steps into the centre and set twice to each other.

73—80 Ladies turn right arms for four bars, then left arms to finish facing opposite men.

81—88 All set.

89—96 All turn right arms for four bars, then left arms to finish men in centre facing each other, ladies on opposite sides.

97—104   Men set to each other.

105—112   Men turn right arms for four bars, then left arms to finish facing their own partners who are still on opposite sides.

113—120   All set to own partners.

121—128   All turn own partners.

THE LANCERS AND QUADRILLES

As well as the twelve 'home-grown' dances, there are two continental-bred introductions, which, with nearly two hundred years of dancing history in Scotland behind them, should be known to all country dancers. Although they have faded from the scene somewhat over the past thirty years, there are now distinct signs that they are regaining popularity, especially at dances held in the country areas.

But be warned! These dances enjoy many local variations and they are danced with varying degrees of vigour.

THE LANCERS

First Figure.

Bars

1—8   Introduction — Honour partners and corners.

9—16   First lady and third man advance into centre, honour each other and swing.

17—24   First and third couples change places, first couple passing between third couple, and return to original places, third couple passing between first couple.

25—32   All set to and swing corners.

33—104   Repeat bars 9—32 three times, with third, second and fourth ladies and appropriate men leading.

Second Figure.

1—8   Introduction — Honour partners and corners.

9—16   First and third couples join inner hands and advance and retire; advance again; men turn their partners round to face them (ladies standing back to back in the centre, curtsey).

17—24   First and third couples set to partners and swing, finishing in original places; first and third couples join hands with corners to face across the dance.

25—32   All advance, retire and swing partners back to original places.

33—56   Repeat bars 9—32 with second and fourth couples leading.

57—104   Repeat bars 9—56.

Third Figure.

Bars

1—8   Introduction — Honour partners and corners.

9—16   All ladies advance, curtsey and stand while men advance between them, cross wrists and clasp hands of opposite man; ladies link arms with adjoining men.

17—24   All circle left, breaking off to original places.

25—32   All men advance and retire; advance and place left hands on opposite men's shoulders.

33—40   Men place right arms around partners' waists; cartwheel anti-clockwise and return to original places.

41—64   Repeat bars 9—32.

65—72   Men place right arms around partner's waists (partners facing opposite way); cartwheel clockwise (men going backwards, ladies forwards) and return to original positions.

Fourth Figure.

1—8   Introduction — Honour partners and corners.

9—16   First and third couples visit (quick waltz step) the couple on their right, acknowledge them and likewise visit and

116

acknowledge the couples on their left before returning to places.

17—24 First and fourth couples and second and third couple dance right hands across right round and left hands back.

25—32 First and fourth couples and second and third couples link arms, circle left and break back to original positions.

33—56 Repeat bars 9—32 but this time first couple dance with second couple and third couple with fourth couple.

57—104 Repeat bars 9—56 with second and fourth couples leading.

Fifth Figure

Introductory chord only.

1—16 Grand chain.

17—24 First couple perform a sweeping turn and dance into their partners' place facing outwards; second, then fourth couples fall in behind first couple, third couple stand still, thus forming two lines, ladies on their partners' right.

25—32 All walk three steps to partners' side of the dance (ladies passing in front of men) and return three steps to own sides.

33—40 First couple, followed by second, fourth and third couples, cast off down the outside of the dance and lead up the inside, finishing in two lines, ladies facing men.

41—48 With hands joined, lines advance, retire, advance again and swing partners back to original places.

49—192 Repeat bars 1—48 three times, second, third and fourth couples leading in turn.

193—208 Grand chain.

THE QUADRILLES

First Figure

Bars

1—8   Introduction — Honour partners and corners.

9—16   First and third couples dance rights and lefts.

17—24   First and third couples set to partners and swing.

25—32   First and third couples perform a Ladies chain.

33—40   First and third couples with promenade hold dance to opposite sides of the dance and return with half rights and lefts to original places.

41—72   Second and fourth couples repeat bars 9—40.

Second Figure

1—8   Introduction — Honour partners and corners.

9—16   First and third couples advance, retire, and dance to opposite corners.

17—24   First and third couples advance, retire and return to original places.

25—32   First and third couple set to partners and swing.

33—56   Second and fourth couples repeat bars 9—32.

57—104 Repeat bars 9—56.

Third Figure

1—8   Introduction — Honour partners and corners.

9—16   First lady and third man cross over right hands. Cross back left hands and, retaining hold, grasp partner by right hands, all four finishing facing in opposite directions across the dance.

17—24   All four set in a line. Men lead partners round to opposite places.

25—32   First lady and third man advance, retire, advance and retire again.

33—40   First and third couples advance, retire and dance half rights and lefts back to original places.

41—136   Third, second and fourth ladies in turn with their opposite men repeat bars 9—40.

Fourth Figure.

1—8   Introduction — Honour partners and corners.

9—16   First couple advance, retire and advance again. First man returns to his own side while first lady moves to the left of third man.

17—24   Third man with first and third ladies advances, retires and advances again, handing ladies over to first man.

25—32   First man with first and third ladies advances, retires and advances again. Third man comes forward and all join hands in a circle.

33—40   All half-circle to opposite places and return with half rights and lefts to original positions.

41—136   Third, second and fourth couples repeat bars 9—40 in turn.

Fifth Figure

1—8   Introduction — Honour partners and corners.

9—16   All join hands in a circle, advance, retire and swing partners to original positions.

17—24   First and third couples advance and retire and taking promenade hold dance to opposite sides.

25—32   Ladies' chain.

33—40   First and third couples advance and retire and taking promenade hold return to original places.

41—72   Repeat bars 9—40 with second and fourth couples leading.

73—136   repeat bars 9—72.

Sixth Figure.

No Introduction

1—8   All ladies advance into centre and retire. All men do likewise.

9—16   All set to corners and swing corners.

17—24   Taking promenade hold with corners all dance round in a clockwise direction, finishing with men returning to their original positions and their corner ladies taking up new positions on their corner mens' right.

25—32   All join hands in a circle, advance, retire and swing partners.

33—128   Repeat bars 1—32 three times.

NOTES ON THE LANCERS AND QUADRILLES

Forget your pas de basque and country dance travelling steps; use a walking step for your progressions.   Setting is done by stepping, to the right side first, for three steps before taking another three steps, this time to the left, to return to the original position. Easier on the carpet than the earlier twelve dances, they are ideal for home entertainment.

GLOSSARY OF DANCING TERMS

CARTWHEEL. Partners join together, either by taking inside hands or by a waist grip. Depending on the situation, either the ladies or the men join their free hands together so that the couples represent the spokes of a wheel. All then dance round.

CAST OFF. Normally done down the dance; the lady turns by the right and man by the left to dance behind the other dancers. Unless the dancing couple are to return to their positions, other dancers must step up to fill the vacated places otherwise the entire set would be forced down the dancing area.

CHAIN. Normally done in a circle formation with men going anti-clockwise and ladies clockwise. Partners face each other and cross over giving right hands, then continue advancing alternating left and right hands as they meet the oncoming men and ladies.

CORNERS. The most confusing of all terms. Both the dancing man and the dancing lady have identifiable corners. In a longwise set, the dancing lady's first and second corners are the second man and the third man respectively. The dancing man's first and second corners are the third lady and the second lady respectively. If then the dancing couple are facing their first or their second corners, they are inevitably standing back to back and in a diagonal line with the selected corner.

HANDS ROUND AND HANDS ACROSS. The term 'hands' denotes the number of dancers and not the number of digit-carrying appendages on display. Thus, 'eight hands round' means eight people are dancing slip step in a circle, all hands joined. 'Four hands across' means that four dancers are joining right hands to dance travelling step in a circle for a given distance, e.g. half-way round. 'And Back again' means returning to original position but with the left hands joined.

LADIES' CHAIN. This movement involves two couples standing opposite each other. The ladies cross over with right hands, turn the opposite men with left hands, cross back again giving right hands and turn their partners left hands back to original place.

PETRONELLA TURN. The name given to a turn using setting step. The complete sequence for a lady is to turn by the right into the centre of the set facing down the dance where she sets before turning again to her partner's place where she sets again. Another turn takes her into the centre of the set facing up the dance where, after setting, she returns to her original place and once more sets. The man also commences by turning to the right but at the end of his first quarter petronella turn he is, of course, facing up the the dance.

POUSSETTE. An attractive progression involving normally, but not always,two couples, which allows the dancing couple to move one place down the dance. The couples involved join hands with their partners and using setting steps move to the sidelines, turn up or down the dance as approppriate, turn into the centre of the dance where they turn again before falling back into their new positions. The dancing couple making the progression always start the poussette by moving out to the men's side of the dance, while the couple to move up move out to the ladies's side.

PROMENADE HOLD. For use when travelling. Side by side, the couple hold their arms crossed in front of them at waist level and join right hand with right hand and left hand with left hand.

RIGHTS AND LEFTS. Normally done in a square formation by two couples standing initially on their own sides of the dance, both couples starting at the same time. Partners cross with each other giving right hands, they then give left hands to the man or lady they have been standing beside as they dance up or down the opposite sides of the dance, then right hands to their partners and once more left hands to the man or lady they have been standing beside.

FORMATIONS

Longwise Set
(e.g. Petronella)

Music

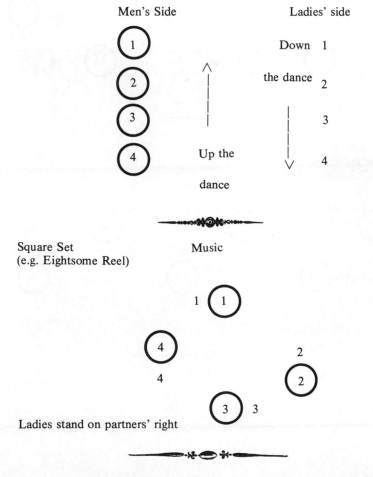

Men's Side   Ladies' side

1   Down 1

2   the dance 2

3   3

4   Up the   4

dance

Square Set   Music
(e.g. Eightsome Reel)

1   1

4

4

2

2

3   3

Ladies stand on partners' right

123

Round the Room in Threes
(e.g. Dashing White Sergeant)

L $\overset{\longrightarrow}{\longleftarrow}$ (M)　　　(M) $\overset{\cdots\rightarrow}{\longleftarrow}$ L　　　(M) $\overset{\longrightarrow}{\longleftarrow}$ L

(M) $\overset{\longleftarrow}{\longrightarrow}$ L　　　L $\overset{\longrightarrow}{\longleftarrow}$ (M)　　　L $\overset{\longrightarrow}{\longleftarrow}$ (M)

L $\overset{\longrightarrow}{\longleftarrow}$ (M)　　　(M) $\overset{\longrightarrow}{\longleftarrow}$ L　　　(M) $\overset{\longrightarrow}{\longleftarrow}$ L

Round the Room in Twos
(e.g. Circassian Circle)

(M) $\overset{\longrightarrow}{\longleftarrow}$ L　　　(M) $\overset{\longrightarrow}{\longleftarrow}$ L　　　(M) $\overset{\longrightarrow}{\longleftarrow}$ L

L $\overset{\longrightarrow}{\longleftarrow}$ (M)　　　L $\overset{\longrightarrow}{\longleftarrow}$ (M)　　　L $\overset{\longrightarrow}{\longleftarrow}$ (M)

Four Couple Progressive
(e.g. La Tempete)

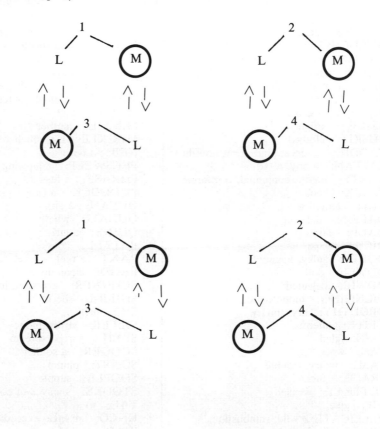

GLOSSARY

AIBLINS: perhaps
ANEUCH: enough
BAULD: brave, impetuous
BAWD: a hare
BIDE: remain, dwell
BOB: dance
BOGILL: a ghost
BRICHT: bright
BUSKIT: clothed
CADDIE: a servant lad, a ragamuffin
CALLAN: a boy, a lad
CANTY: merry, contented, comfortable
CLEEK: hook
CUIT: an ankle
DAFFIN: dallying
DAUR: dare
DICHT: wipe
DORTY: sulky, haughty
DOWFF: dull
DOWIE: dejected
DRINGING: monotonous
DROUTHY: dry, thirsty
ETTLE: attempt
FAIN: glad
FAN: when
FASH: worry, trouble
FRAISE: fuss
FUTTRAT: weasel
GIE: give
HELLICATE: wild, rumbustious
HINMOST: final, hindmost
HYNE: to a distance
ILK: each, every
JALOUSE: imagine, suspect

JIMP: short, slender, neat
KEEK: glance, peep
LAITIS: manners
LEUCH: laugh
LOUP: leap
MANTIE: a cloak, outer garment
MAUN: must
MINNIE: mother
MUCKLE: big, much
NEB: a nose
PEESWEEP: a lapwing
PHRASE: a fuss
PUDDOCK: a frog
QUEAN: a girl
QUHAIR: where
QUINE: a girl
RAFFEL: doeskin
RANT: a reel, a revel
REDD: clean up
SCUNNER: aversion, loathing
SHIRRA: sheriff
SIC: such
SILLER: silver, money
SKIRL: shriek, scream
SODGER: a soldier
SONSY: plump
SOOPLE: supple
STOOKS: sheaves of corn set up to dr
TAE: to
UNCO: strange, exceedingly
WAD: would
WAE: sad
WHAUP: a curlew
WIMPLE: ripple

LUATH PRESS
GUIDES TO
WESTERN SCOTLAND

SOUTH WEST SCOTLAND: Tom Atkinson.

A guidebook to the best of Kyle, Carrick, Galloway, Dumfries-shire, Kirkcudbrightshire and Wigtownshire.
This lovely land of hills, moors and beaches is bounded by the Atlantic and the Solway. Steeped in history and legend, still unspoiled, it is a land whose peace and grandeur are at least comparable to the Highlands.
Legends, history and loving descriptions by a local author make this an essential book for all who visit — or live in — the country of Robert Burns.
ISBN 0 946847 04 9. Paperback. £2:00p.

THE LONELY LANDS Tom Atkinson.

A guide book to Inveraray, Kintyre, Glen Coe, Loch Awe, Loch Lomond, Cowal, the Kyles of Bute, and all of central Argyll.
All the glories of Argyll are described in this book. From Dumbarton to Campbeltown there is a great wealth of beauty. It is a quiet and lonely land, a land of history and legend, a land of unsurpassed glory. Tom Atkinson describes it all, writing with deep insight of the land he loves. There could be no better guide to its beauties and history. Every visitor to this country of mountains and lochs and lonely beaches will find that enjoyment is enhanced by reading this book.
ISBN 0 946847 10 3. Paperback. Price: £2:00p.

ROADS TO THE ISLES. Tom Atkinson. A guide-book to Scotland's Far West, including Morar, Moidart, Morvern and Ardnamurchan.

This is the area lying to the west and north-west of Fort William. It is a land of still unspoiled loveliness, of mountain, loch and silver sands. It is a vast, quiet land of peace and grandeur. Legend, history and vivid description by an author who loves the area and knows it intimately make this book essential to all who visit this Highland wonderland.
ISBN 0 946487 01 4. Paperback. £1:80p.

THE

JOLLY

BEGGARS

or

LOVE & LIBERTY A Cantata

With A Facsimile of A Hand-
Written Copy Prepared by
The Poet Himself.

ROBERT
BURNS

The Jolly Beggars

Robert Burns

Luath Press

THE BLEW BLANKET LIBRARY

The Blew (or Blue) Blanket was the privileged insignia of the craftsmen of Edinburgh in the time of James III. It was pledged to them by Privy Seal in 1482 when the craftsmen of the city, together with the merchants and other loyal subjects, marched on Edinburgh Castle and freed their King. It remained their insignia for centuries, and one of the original Blew Blankets is today in the Museum of Antiquities in Edinburgh.

The Blew Blanket Library is a collection of new books on Scotland by Scottish writers. Its aim is to provide a forum where writer-craftsmen of all types can display their wares in the context of Scotland today.

Already available in *The Blew Blanket Library.*

THE CROFTING YEARS. Francis Thompson.

A remarkable and moving study of crofting in the Highlands and Islands. It tells of the bloody conflicts a century ago when the crofters and their families faced all the forces of law and order and demanded a legal status and security of tenure, and of how gunboats cruised the Western Isles in Government's classic answer.

Life in the crofting townships is described with great insight and affection. Food, housing, healing and song are all dealt with. But the book is no nostalgic longing for the past. It looks to the future and argues that crofting must be carefully nurtured as a reservoir of potential strength for an uncertain future.

Francis Thompson lives and works in Stornoway. His life has been intimately bound up with the crofters, and he well knows of what he writes.

ISBN 0 946487 06 5. Paperback Price: £3:00p.

TALL TALES FROM AN ISLAND. Peter Macnab.

These tales come from the island of Mull, but they could just as well come from anywhere in the Highlands or Islands.

Witches, ghosts, warlocks and fairies abound, as do stories of the people, their quiet humour and their abiding wit. A book to dip into, laugh over and enthuse about. Out of this great range of stories a general picture appears of an island people, stubborn and strong in adversity, but warm and co-operative and totally wedded to their island way of life. It is a clear picture of a microcosmic society perfectly adapted to an environment that, in spite of its great beauty, can be harsh and unforgiving.

Peter Macnab was born and grew up on Mull, and he knows and loves every inch of it. Not for him the 'superiority' of the incomer who makes joke cardboard figures of the island people and their ways. He presents a rounded account of Mull and its people.

ISBN 0 946487. Paperback. Price: £3:95p.

THE EDGE OF THE WOOD. Alan Bold.

This is Alan Bold's first solo collection of short stories, and it is an impressive one. Here we have tales of the Scottish reality of today, tales told by a master craftsman. It is a fine collection, ranging from murder in a Scottish village to a Black Hole in Space, from a man's love for his dog to a young poet's first love and first poem. One of Scotland's foremost writers of today, Alan Bold has produced a collection of short stories which illustrate, through the eye of an artist, many of Scotland's current problems and contradictions.
ISBN 0 946487 08 1. Paperback. Price £4:25p

THE JOLLY BEGGARS OR LOVE AND LIBERTY.

Robert Burns. A facsimile of the original handwritten copy by Burns himself, with the poet's corrections.
This unusual volume contains not only the original text, but also the printed text on facing pages, and another text with glossary. It contains all the songs and music, and they are newly illustrated by John Hampson, a young Scottish artist of great promise. There is a long Introduction by Tom Atkinson, and an Essay on *Poetry, Politics and Forgetfullness* by William Neil, himself a poet of South-west Scotland. Although but little known today, *Love and Liberty* contains some of Robert Burns's most brilliant poetry and most lively songs. It was Scotland's poet at the height of his genius and power.
This Volume should certainly be on the shelves of every lover of Robert Burns.
ISBN 0 946487 02 2. Casebound. Price £8:00p.

WILD PLACES. William Neill.

Publication of these new poems and broadsheets by William Neill marks a very important step in contemporary Scottish letters. Writing in English, Scots and Gaelic, and translating between them, William Neill brings a strongly disciplined vision to bear on his native land. The lyricism and freedom of his language is matched by the beauty of his imagery, and to that imagery he brings the fruit of Scotland's three linguistic cultures. From such a synthesis has sprung poetry of a strength and virility rarely matched.

ISBN 0 046487 11 1. Paperback. £5:00p.

NEW BOOKS FROM LUATH PRESS

WALKS IN THE CAIRNGORMS. Ernest Cross.

The Cairngorms are the highest uplands in Britain, and walking there introduces you to sub-arctic scenery found nowhere else. This book provides a selection of walks in a splendid and magnificent countryside — there are rare birds, animals and plants, geological curiosities, quiet woodland walks, unusual excursions in the mountains. Ernest Cross has written an excellent guidebook to these things. Not only does he have an intimate knowledge of what he describes, but he loves it all deeply, and this shows.

ISBN 0 946487 09 X Paperback. £1:80p.

THE SCOT AND HIS OATS. G.W. Lockhart.

A survey of the part played by oats and oatmeal in Scottish history, legend, romance and the Scottish character.

Sowing and mowing, stooking and stacking, milling and cooking, they are all in this book. Wallace Lockhart's research has carried him from Froissart to Macdiarmid, and his recipes range from an oatmeal *aperitif* to oatmeal candy. His stories about oats traverse the world from Mafeking to Toronto.

ISBN 0 946487 05 7. Paperback. Price £1:50p.

POEMS TO BE READ ALOUD: *A Victorian Drawing Room Entertainment.* Selected and with an Introduction by Tom Atkinson.

A very personal selection of poems specially designed for all those who believe that the world is full of people who long to hear you declaim such as these. The Entertainment ranges from an unusual and beautiful *Love Song* translated from the Sanskrit, to the drama of *The Shooting of Dan McGrew* and *The Green Eye of the Little Yellow God,* to the bathos of *Trees* and the outrageous bawdiness of *Eskimo Nell.* Altogether, a most unusual and amusing selection.

ISBN 0 946487 00 6. Paperback. Price £1:80p.